SIDE CHICKOLOGY
WHY MEN & WOMEN CHEAT
Understanding, Avoiding, & Recovering from Infidelity

KEITH A. BATTLE
Author of *A Second Chance: Grace for the Broken*

ISBN: 978-1-54396-153-9
E-Book ISBN: 978-1-54396-146-1

ENDORSEMENTS

"I disliked reading Christian books on marriage because I could not identify with their lack of vulnerability. I needed a book where the author was transparent about his own struggles and offered me hope on how I could turn the page in my marriage. That's exactly what you get in Side Chickology. Keith, lifts up the window shade of his heart and allows you to peek inside his marriage to view his failures and the fun he and Vicki now regularly enjoy. Get your copy of Side Chickology. The practical wisdom will help your marriage heal from broken trust and it will keep you from breaking trust as you invest in your marriage."

– Dr. Johnny Parker
Author of Renovating Your Marriage: Room By Room

"Everyone needs this inoculation from adultery before, during or after it occurs. Keith Battle's voice of warning about adultery and encouragement of reconciliation is a timely read... In an immoral world, Side Chickology is that voice keeping us from harm and healing us if we have been injured."

– Douglas Weiss Ph.D. Psychologist, Author.

Pastor Keith Battle's book is insightful, challenging, encouraging and powerful. It will give guidance and solutions to anyone seeking directionwith this all too common issue.

– Pastor John K. Jenkins, Sr.
First Baptist Church of Glenarden, Maryland

CONTENTS

ACKNOWLEDGEMENTS

None of us succeed at anything without the support of others. I am so blessed to have so many people that have helped me to complete this book, that time and space won't allow me to thank them all. Some have just encouraged me with their words to get this done. Others have inspired me to finish with their stories of relational pain and triumph. Although many will go unmentioned in this note of thanks, God knows what you did, and may He bless you in ways that I never could.

Special thanks to the team that help to put this project together. To my outstanding primary editors, Julie Strauss-Gabel and Keidi Keating. To Sharita Slayton for your diligence in combing through the manuscript to make sure it was sound.

To my graphic designers Hugo Fernandez and Dino Marino for the cover and layout design respectively.

To every one of you that purchased this book, told others about it, and even bought a copy for a friend or two. Thank you so much. Your support means a lot.

To my church family, Zion Church. Thanks for your patience with me as I often played hooky from church in order to get this done.

To my Quantum Leap Mastermind accountability flight group. Thanks for not letting me excuse my way out of getting to the finish line.

To my Woodmore Pinochle Club family. Thank you for providing me with a competitive but loving, supportive, and safe outlet.

To my Monopoly Game brothers, Darrell, Kevin, and James. Thanks for the laughs, arguments, music, memories, and the competition. "We may throw the dice, but the Lord determines how they fall." Proverbs 16:33 (NLT) Ha!

To my family – Carsen, Kendall, Asa, & Asha. I'm humbled that God gave me the responsibility of being a father and grandfather. I'm also grateful that God has graciously kept our family together.

To my wife Vicki. Our marriage has experienced mountaintops, valleys, and everything in between over 3 decades. As our journey continues, may our story inspire others.

Finally, Lord, I thank You that although the Apostle Paul wrote 1 Timothy 1:16, it's true of me as well.

"But God had mercy on me so that Christ Jesus could use me as a prime example of his great patience with even the worst sinners. Then others will realize that they, too, can believe in him and receive eternal life."

Keith A. Battle

INTRODUCTION

57 percent of men and 54 percent of women admit to committing infidelity in a relationship they've had.[1] That's an interesting and compelling statistic given the fact that a respected therapist friend of mine says that 95% of persons guilty of unfaithfulness, when confronted with their infidelity by their mates, initially deny it. Therefore, it stands to reason that the cases of infidelity in relationships are probably higher than those in the stats provided above.

In "The State of Affairs", Esther Perel states that, "Because there is no universally agreed-upon definition of what constitutes infidelity, estimates of its prevalence among American couples vary widely, ranging from 26 to 70 percent for women and from 33 to 75 percent for men."[2]

In the world of professional & pastoral counseling, we have definitely seen society's marital commitment level move to a place where 100% fidelity is more of the exception than the rule. Because there is so much opportunity to cheat in our world, whether it's a full-blown physical/sexual affair, or an emotional affair, or a virtual affair via technology and pornography, or flirting on social media or via text messages, having a completely monogamous relationship has become terribly challenging.

I wish I could say that I've been 100 percent faithful to Vicki, my beautiful wife of nearly 30 years, but that wouldn't be veracious. I know what it's like to cross the line. Ironically, it is one of the reasons why I feel qualified to write this book. I know the pain, shame, and devastation caused by perfidy first hand, and I know the arduous journey and the blissful benefits of recovery and rebuilding. So, although I can write on this subject empathically, I will not assuage how serious a matter cheating is.

WHY THIS BOOK?

Back in the late spring of 2015, I shared a message with the Church that I pastor entitled, "Side Chickology". That message was so popular that several years later, I am still getting comments about it. It seemed to clearly hit a cultural nerve regarding a topic that's not always addressed with candor in Church Sermons. Here's a link where you can view the message at anytime - http://zionlandover.com/sermon/293-side-chickology

The response to that message caused me to do some praying and reflecting on whether or not to put those thoughts in writing and expand upon them. The answer to those prayers is at your fingertips now.

The stories and analogies in this Book are not about anyone that I know personally. They are all representative and not real. They embody my three decades of experience of working with married couples in counseling as well as nearly three decades of being married.

In addition to the response to the sermon that I gave that initiated this work, I was motivated to write this book for a number of additional reasons. For starters, Vicki and I would admit the majority of our marriage was awful. It was lonely, hurtful, confusing, and depressing for both of us. Thankfully now our marriage is stronger, healthier, happier, and more vibrant than it's ever been and every single tool and practice that we've used to heal, help and strengthen our marriage is in the pages of this book.

Second, I was inspired to write this book because of the fact that I come from a long history of divorce in my family. My mother was raised in a family of 6 children, and my father in a family of 8, and only 4 of those 14 children were married to one person for a lifetime. In fact, my parents were married a combined 5 times and that reality in my life and family made me want to break that cycle and stay in my marriage even in times when I felt that leaving would've made me much happier. It was my conviction that family continuity was more important than individual preferences that made me stay even when I thought things would never get better. I just believed in family that much. Yet to my surprise, God blessed my marriage in ways that I never dreamed possible, and for that, I am grateful.

I also wrote this book to heighten the awareness of some of the causes of infidelity. If we don't know why something painful happened or could happen to us, we're more susceptible to it than we are when we're equipped with knowledge and insight regarding it.

Finally, I'm writing this book because, in the 31 years that I have been involved in Ministry, I have seen my share of couples that have been in desperate need of hope and tools to repair their shattered relationships. Some I've been able to help and see great healing and success, others, in spite of my best efforts, continued down a path of disintegration and ultimately divorce. I mention this because I don't have a magic wand to miraculously heal marriages, nor is this book a panacea for any and every suffering union. Marriage is hard work, and staying married is a lot harder than getting married. But it's worth the work.

This book will not be everyone's story and it will not fit everyone's experience perfectly. Infidelity is such an expansive topic, that I cannot help but to address it with broad strokes. To attempt to write a book on this subject with detail, using various relational nuances and circumstances would require volumes, not chapters.

I think it's also important to note that some of what I write in this book is influenced by my Christian beliefs; however, the content of this book will help people of all religious beliefs and practices as well as those who have no particular religious persuasion.

Although it is not my goal to proselytize anyone with this book, I do believe that the regular practice of prayer and faith and obedience to spiritual truth have a significant impact on the strength of our relationships. For this reason, I'll be making reference to biblical literature at various points in this book. In fact, you may be surprised to know that the Bible actually has a number of things to say about Side Chicks and infidelity.

My hope and prayer is that this book will make an impact on how we view marriage, and how hard we're willing to work to do the things necessary to protect it.

Keith A. Battle

DISCLAIMER:

The term "Side Chickology" was created to reference the study of a mistress – how she operates and how she gains access to monogamous relationships. The term is not intended to be disparaging or sexist. Indeed, women aren't the only gender who engage in infidelity. There are men who are what I would call "Side Slicks" and I'll mention them as well in this book. Meanwhile, the main focus of this book is to educate couples regarding the things that make the fidelity of their relationships vulnerable and to provide tools to protect their most prized **union**.

CHAPTER 1:

ATTENTION DEFICIT DISORDER

Attention deficit disorder (ADD) is a weakness in the brain's ability to focus on important sensory information. An attention deficit may also impact the brain's ability to filter out information that's not important.[1]

Anyone that knows me well is aware that I am an advocate for the world of Mental Health. I genuinely care about people who live with mental illness, or have learning challenges.

I mention those things because I don't mean to use the ADD terminology in a flippant or degrading way. However, I think it's ironic that at the foundation of many committed relationships that end up experiencing infidelity is something that I call relational ADD.

So often, people just don't feel like they're being recognized, honored, valued, and treasured in the relationship, and this leads to them hungering for that attention outside of the relationship.

THE PATTERN

More often than not within relationships, things tend to grow cold and distant as the marriage naturally atrophies over time into gradual stages of isolation. Especially nowadays, when so much creativity and energy is put into the marriage proposal and engagement, and often even more work is put into having spectacular wedding ceremonies and honeymoons, that there appears to be a significant drop off in creativity, energy, and effort invested in strengthening the marriage. This leads to the natural regression of a marriage relationship that doesn't intentionally labor to move against the grain of relational degeneration.

Furthermore, marriages tend to naturally drift into isolation and distance because, for the most part, everything in our lives pulls us apart and not together. We have hectic professional schedules. Busy commutes to and from our jobs. We bring employment-related projects home, whether it's a proposal for work, an assignment from our post-graduate degree program, or our real estate license studies. It's the papers we have to grade and the lesson plans we have to put together for the students at the school where we teach. It's the time-sensitive project that we're laboring on for our Department that demands our very best attention.

Then of course we have our exercise schedules. There's yoga class and Zumba class. There's the 12-week weight loss boot camp that we signed up for, for the 3rd time because we have successfully lost and re-gained the weight each time.

Then there are our community-related activities, homeowner's association meetings, "Meet me at the Polls" voter registration work, and our role as the team parent for our kids' sports.

We have our favorite television shows and events that aren't necessarily of interest to our spouse. So, we typically watch them alone while our mate is in another part of the house doing whatever they're doing.

Many reading this book are involved in church or social clubs that consume some of our week, and oh, we can't forget about the greatest blessings/marital dividers, the children.

They have their own needs, schedules, activities, demands, etc. Pick-ups and drop-offs. Doctor's appointments and overnight parties. School functions and school projects. The work never ends.

In fact, I call the time in marriage relationships before children, the "BC Days". Some of you may remember the Before Children days, when you could date spontaneously, without having to secure a babysitter and pack a baby bag with special instructions for the sitter.

The days when you could have sex together anytime and anywhere in the house and not have to wait until all the kids were sound asleep and your bedroom door was securely locked.

The "BC Days" were when husbands felt like they were their wives' number one priority, before they dropped uninformed in the priority rankings somewhere behind the children.

The "BC Days" were when wives had enough energy to work, keep the house relatively clean, cook a creative and healthy dinner, and still have the time and energy to have sex with their husbands, go to the gym, the store, and read books. (Probably makes you smile and chuckle just reading that.)

But then came "Junior" and/or "Princess" and now we're in the "AD Days" (After Dependents Days). The wife's work is never done, her home is less than tidy, the dinner consists of whatever can be made fast (healthy or not). After helping with homework, breaking up fights, picking up children from practice, giving baths, and tucking kiddos into bed, she feels like collapsing in the hallway between her children's room and her own room. Just as she musters up barely enough strength to will her exhausted body into the bed, her husband winks at her, hoping tonight is his lucky night for an evening rendezvous.

Or worse, instead of even asking his wife, because he feels bereft from hearing "no" to his requests for sexual intimacy so many times, he goes into his man cave and looks at pornography and masturbates to avoid "bothering" her or being rejected by her. (More about this in Chapter 2.)

Given the fact that she feels unsupported and under-appreciated for all of her professional and domestic labor, she feels like it's insensitive for her husband to ask for sex when he hasn't even called her at any point in the day to express his love and appreciation for her. Some women reading this are so sick and angry about what I just wrote that they are considering putting this book down now to confront their husbands regarding whether or not that "Man-Cave Behavior" is true. But please don't do that. We have a long way to go, and I'll tell you all you need to know about the Man Cave in Chapter 2.

Meanwhile, if you'd ask either the husband or wife at this stage in their relationship, how the marriage is going, she'll probably say, "All he wants is sex." And he's likely to sheepishly say, "We have an intimacy problem in our marriage", because married men often develop unhealthy feelings of shame around their sexual desires. But he really wants to say, "She never wants to have sex."

And herein lies a serious problem, because contrary to popular belief, men don't just need sex physiologically to be content, although a sexual orgasm is a feeling that's hard to match. Sex also helps us to feel close to our wives. It closes the distance gap, and it makes us feel like we're a priority. So, when a man doesn't get to have sexual intimacy with his wife, he doesn't just miss out on an opportunity for pleasure, he also doesn't feel close to his wife. He doesn't feel like he's a priority, especially if he's witnessed the length that his wife will go to comfort and nurture their children, which in turn angers him about the situation.

At the same time, women ideally need to feel close to their husbands in order to want to be with them sexually; otherwise, they feel like they're just performing a wifely duty. This is what I call "Duty-Booty".

Notice the relational chasm and complex cycle that the couple now faces. There's a feeling of distance in the relationship that reveals itself in the inactivity in the bedroom. This intimacy gap is difficult to close because remember, while the husband needs sex to feel close, the wife needs closeness to be interested in sex.

Since she doesn't feel close, she says, "No, not tonight." He, in turn, self-pleasures, and ultimately becomes addicted to non-relational, non-connecting, pleasure-based sex. He stops, asking, and therefore, the bed becomes only a resting place and not a place of intimacy, closeness and romance, and the isolation gap widens.

Now, both begin to throw themselves and their energy continually away from each other and into the people and things that either need them or feed them (bringing them satisfaction). In many instances, the husband becomes a workaholic or a golf-aholic or an alcoholic or a porn-aholic or any other-holic, whether it's socially acceptable or not, that brings him some pleasure, reward, and satisfaction. He does this often because even though he feels like he's losing in his marriage, this other world gives him an opportunity to get some "wins".

Simultaneously, the wife often throws herself deeper into her career or her children. She gets the kids involved in things that require more and more of her time, energy, and commitment. And this is where she's drawn because she feels like she's losing in her marriage, while her "wins" are coming from watching her children grow, enjoy life, develop, and succeed.

So now the photograph of she and her husband that was once prominent in her cubicle at work has been overshadowed by the "I luv U Mommy" drawing from her 6- year-old and the report card of her 4th-grader with all As and one B. Even though she'd rather showcase her marriage more, that's not where she's winning.

And ironically, just as a wife may begin to internally dislike the people and places that are getting all of her husband's attention, the husband may secretly begin to be jealous of his own children who seem to have *taken* his wife's energy, time, attention, and love away from him.

This couple is now officially Side-Chick vulnerable.

THE MARRIED SIDE-CHICK

Check out this interesting story in the Old Testament Book of Proverbs.

PROVERBS 7

1
Follow my advice, my son;
always treasure my commands.
2
Obey my commands and live!
Guard my instructions as you guard your own eyes.

3
Tie them on your fingers as a reminder
Write them deep within your heart.
4
Love wisdom like a sister;
make insight a beloved member of your family.
5
Let them protect you from an affair with an immoral woman,
from listening to the flattery of a promiscuous woman.
6
While I was at the window of my house,
looking through the curtain,
7
I saw some naive young men,
and one in particular who lacked common sense.
8
He was crossing the street near the house of an immoral woman,
strolling down the path by her house.
9
It was at twilight, in the evening,
as deep darkness fell.
10
The woman approached him,
seductively dressed and sly of heart.
11
She was the brash, rebellious type,
never content to stay at home.
12
She is often in the streets and markets,
soliciting at every corner.
13
She threw her arms around him and kissed him,
and with a brazen look she said,
14
"I've just made my peace offerings
and fulfilled my vows.
15
You're the one I was looking for!
I came out to find you, and here you are!
16
My bed is spread with beautiful blankets,
with colored sheets of Egyptian linen.
17
I've perfumed my bed
with myrrh, aloes, and cinnamon.

18
Come, let's drink our fill of love until morning.
Let's enjoy each other's caresses,
19
for my husband is not home.
He's away on a long trip.
20
He has taken a wallet full of money with him
and won't return until later this month."
21
So she seduced him with her pretty speech
and enticed him with her flattery.
22
He followed her at once,
like an ox going to the slaughter.
He was like a stag caught in a trap,
23
awaiting the arrow that would pierce its heart.
He was like a bird flying into a snare,
little knowing it would cost him his life.
24
So listen to me, my sons,
and pay attention to my words.
25
Don't let your hearts stray away toward her.
Don't wander down her wayward path.
26
For she has been the ruin of many;
many men have been her victims.
27
Her house is the road to the grave.
Her bedroom is the den of death.2

Wow! That story *never* gets old to me. In fact, I recommend that anyone struggling with the temptation to engage in an inappropriate relationship with someone else's spouse spend several weeks each day reading Proverbs chapters 5, 6, and 7. It's pretty powerful stuff indeed.

One of the ironies of this Proverbs 7 story is that *this* "Side-Chick" is married. She's somebody's wife, but she's seducing another man while her husband is away on some kind of trip.

Many times, when we think of "Side-Chicks" we think of single women involved in relationships with men who are already in a committed relationship with someone else. But again, in this case, the Side Chick in Proverbs 7 is married.

And a casual reading of the story would suggest that she may be suffering from a little relational ADD, given the fact that her husband is away from home for an extended period of time without her.

Relationships that involve a spouse whose work schedule keeps him or her away from home for extended periods of time are recipes for disaster when it comes to trying to have a faithfully committed marriage. These relationships require lots of intentional and creative ways of connecting and staying "together" while a part. Using technology to see each other and even share sexual intimacy virtually if necessary may be one of the ways of keeping these kinds of relationships protected from infidelity.

When we read this account in Proverbs 7, it serves as a point of emphasis to husbands to consider the notion that we could be unintentionally helping our wives to become a Side Chick by ignoring them and leaving them alone so much.

In 1981, Ray Parker, Jr. wrote a song called, "A Woman Needs Love". Some of you who remember it, will start hearing the melody as you read some of the lyrics below:

A woman needs love, just like you do, hoo
Don't kid yourself, into thinkin' that she don't
She can fool around just like you do, hoo
Unless you give her all the lovin' she wants

Because a woman needs love, just like you do, hoo
Hey, don't kid yourself into thinking that she don't
She can fool around just like you do, hoo
Unless you give her all the lovin' she wants

I tell you one day you'll come home
Early from work [Home from work]
Open up the door
And get your feelings hurt

Now an example to you
Is by the time poor Jack

Returned up the hill
Somebody else
Had been lovin' Jill[3]

Forgive the digression, but hopefully the point was made. I didn't quote the Ray Parker, Jr. song to *justify* infidelity or excuse it. I simply brought up the song to explain the fact that women have needs just like men, and although their needs are often emotional, we all tend to express our deepest emotional needs sexually. Which of course, is why once she gets emotionally close to another man, sexual intercourse is not far away.

Back to Proverbs 7. This married Side-Chick approached this strange man on the street, and her seductive appeals to him to have intercourse with her were too much for him to resist, and we're told that "he followed her at once, like an ox going to the slaughter. He was like a stag caught in a trap… He was like a bird flying into a snare, little knowing it would cost him his life."

That imagery is both amazing and disturbing because it's a reminder of the fact that infidelity may be pleasurable but the cost is far higher than the return.

I'll never forget the first time I heard Pastor Ravi Zacharias say in a sermon that "Sin will take you further than you want go, keep you longer than you want stay, and cost you more than you want to pay." I've seen the profound accuracy of this statement many times over in my life.

Sexual seduction can cause a man to have such an enormous physiological pleasure rush that he is unable to recognize the imminent danger that he's getting himself into.

In fact, a counselor whose work and thinking I greatly admire, once told me that the male brain is wired in such a way that we can recognize and react to female pulchritude faster than we can recognize and react to danger. Imagine the countless men who have walked into things or drove into things because the anatomy of a woman had captured their attention.

In the Proverbs 7 Story, this young man is smitten by the seduction of another's man's wife, and the advice of the sage in this Proverb is, "Don't let your heart stray away towards her. Don't wander down her wayward path." In other words, get her off of your heart and mind and stay off of her street and away from her house. Don't just resist, run!

Now that may seem trite, but one of the greatest strategies that a man can use to avoid being trapped and snared by a Side-Chick is to just intentionally stay away from her. If she's on the elevator, take the steps. If she takes the steps, you get on the elevator. If you work together and she's staying late at work, you go home on time or early if necessary.

Flirtation is all about proximity, whether it's physical or virtual proximity. So, you have to be intentional about not only "staying off of her street," but also staying off of her social media page as well.

During the time that Proverbs 7 was written, if you were going to engage in an inappropriate relationship with someone, you had to geographically be in the same place that they were in. Nowadays, all you need is an Internet connection and a mobile device and you can have an inappropriate relationship with someone in a different time zone and even on a different continent.

I think it's very important to point out here the fact that because sexual temptation is such a powerful and alluring phenomenon, we must never assume that we are strong enough to be constantly around it and victorious over it. The truth is, there are some things that we weren't made to stand up to and sexual temptation is one of them. If you don't walk or run away, and instead try to stand up to it, you may end up lying down with it.

*If you struggle with sexual purity, like most of us, then here's a tool that you can download from our website entitled, "Life's Greatest Battle: Sexual Purity". You can access it now at www.sagacitycompany.com

*Note: I've included affirmations at the conclusion of every chapter. Affirmations are powerful tools used to remind us of our goals and to inspire us towards our highest good. Allow these affirmations to become your own and regularly recite them for your personal motivation.

Affirmations

If a person is not fully single, I will not engage in or pursue an intimate relationship with them. They can't just be estranged from their spouse, or even legally separated. They must be divorced, unmarried, widowed, or never married.

I will make time to give loving attention to my spouse. I will put reminders on my calendar to connect with my spouse and meet his or her physical and emotional needs.

CHAPTER 2:

MAN CAVE SECRETS –
THE MAKING OF AN ADULTERER

Just like the first man in all of human history (Adam) was made from the ground, we men are earthy by nature. We were created from the ground. Women, on the other hand, were created from inside of man. (More about that in Chapter 9).

We men have our origin from the ground. That may be why we love basements in homes so much. Man caves give us seclusion. It's a place to escape from the noise and stress of our house. It can be a den, the garage, a guest bedroom, or any secluded area in our home. It's almost a must for a man's sanity.

In addition to seclusion, another reason why men escape to their man cave is that it's a safe haven from the tension in their relationship. It's a place to get away from arguments with our spouse. It's a place where we're in charge. We've got our music, television, a remote control, our comfortable chair, and for many men, it's where they also have their video game system, beer, wine, snacks, and smoking supplies as well.

Many younger men escape to the man cave to play video games. Others go there to listen to music and unwind. Some go there to work out. Others go just to relax.

Now if you were a fly on a man cave wall, you would also discover that oftentimes man caves are full of dirty little secrets. But before I tell you those secrets, let me tell you how a man ends up spending so much time in his man cave.

"What We Got Here is Failure to Communicate"

That's a famous quote from the 1967 Movie "Cool Hand Luke" starring Paul Newman and Strother Martin. I borrow it for this section of the book because the prelude to isolation in relationships is the inability to effectively communicate.

I love the writings of Gary Smalley on the subject of marriage. His books, humor, insight, and transparency have aided me greatly over the years. One of the things that I learned from Smalley is that there are generally six levels of communication. Marriages that are healthy tend to have communication on all six levels, while marriages that struggle tend to only communicate on two or three of the six levels. Here are Smalley's Six Levels of Communication:[1]

Level 1 is *Small Talk*. It's when we just sort of shoot the breeze with one another. Nothing profound is said; just small talk. How are you doing? Good morning! What's up? Have a nice day, etc.

Level 2 is *Facts*. It's raining outside. The Giants beat the Bears by three points yesterday. The Stock Market had a major fluctuation today. Traffic was heavy on the Interstate this evening.

These first two levels of communication are superficial, non-threatening levels of conversing. Very few arguments start on this level and therefore it's safe but shallow. Unfortunately, many relationships suffer because this is as deep as the interaction goes between the two people, and often, at least one of the persons longs for deeper dialogue.

Level 3 is *Opinions*. This is a risky level of communication because now the conversation moves from the superficial (Small Talk) and the undeniable (Facts) to what a person thinks. This level is risky because there may very well be a disagreement in opinions, which can lead to conflict. There are a lot of relationships that are suffering in the area of communication because once couples hit this land mine level of opinions and they realize it's been the catalyst to arguments and fights, the two people tend to just shut down and cease sharing their opinions with one another. They go back to what I call "survival communication". That is when we only say what needs to be said on the Small Talk and Facts levels to make it from day to day. It goes something like this:

Wife: "Good Morning. Cyndi (daughter) has practice today."

Husband: "Ok…"

Husband: "Roger (Friend) called me and asked if Timmy (Roger's son) could come over and play with Jeffrey (son) today."

Wife: "Ok. Have a nice day."

Husband: "You too."

This level of communication is meant to keep the emotional climate in the home safe because if a shift is made to Level 3 (Opinions) and the wife says, "Well I don't think you should let Timmy come over since Jeffrey is doing so poorly in school." The husband feels like shots have been fired, and his judgment and parenting have been attacked, so he responds, "Well if you'd spend more time with Jeffrey, and stop spending all of your time with Cyndi, maybe his grades would improve. You're the trained educator in this house. How can you let your own son fail in school right under your roof!?" Thus begins World War III.

So again, because couples are often missing some very important communication tools to help them navigate safely and effectively through the difficult terrain of riskier levels of dialogue, they tend to revert back to Levels 1 and 2 just to keep the peace.

Sometimes things get so bad and there's so much hurt, anger, disappointment, and hopelessness, that the couple moves below Levels 1 and 2, and begins to literally function in the house with no communication at all. This is when the marriage is in full-blown "silence violence" as author and therapist Johnny Parker[2] calls it. When the relationship gets to that point, the emotional tension in the home is nerve racking. (I'll share some very important communication tools to help with these challenges in Chapter 12.)

The next three levels of communication are often the ones that separates healthy from unhealthy marriage relationships. Couples who can regularly interact on these levels usually enjoy greater trust and intimacy. They are as follows:

Level 4 is *Feelings*. It's when we're able to express our deepest emotional fears, pain, disappointments, and pleasure with our spouse. For example, "I feel like you're doing too much." Or, "I feel like we need to spend more time together."

Level 5 is *Needs*. Example, "I need to know that no matter what happens you're here to stay. I need to know that you're not here just for the kids."

Level 6 is *Beliefs*. Example, "I believe that our marriage would be far better if we had a regular date night and if we had more fun. I believe I should be your top priority, humanly speaking."

Again, the key to the Six Levels of Communication is the fact that in order for a relationship to be healthy, it needs to be fluent on all six levels. All of our conversations don't need to be on the feelings, needs, or beliefs level. It's okay to shoot the breeze with one another, in fact, the relationship needs times of communicating that's not heavy and deep. However, we need to be able to communicate on all six levels without things turning into a fight.

Unfortunately, many marriages struggle tremendously in the area of communication, and as a consequence, men become regulars in their man caves because they don't feel like they can converse with their wives in a healthy way.

*One of four major relationship vital signs is Communication. I discuss it and the three other vital signs in depth in a message entitled, "Relationship Vital Signs". You can download it here at www.sagacitycompany.com

INSIDE THE MAN CAVE

In fairness, every trip to the man cave is not an attempt to escape the strain of the relationship. The man cave is a respite from multiple challenges. Those challenges include but are not limited to: *parenting, work, financial management, decision-making, weight loss, blood pressure maintenance, stress management, aging parents*, and so on.

But when it comes specifically to the marriage relationship, the man cave can become a dark place for a man, because it's often the feelings of pain and rejection or the lack of appreciation, love, and support that drives him there. Particularly if he's feeling sexually deprived, he'll be tempted to turn his man cave into a virtual replacement for the sexual intimacy he's missing in his marriage.

Now I'm aware that there are hundreds of thousands if not millions of women in the world who feel sexually deprived as well. Women who have not been sexually pursued by their husbands in weeks, months, and even years in some cases. When they try to initiate sexual intimacy with their husbands their husbands turn them down claiming fatigue, stress, or a number of other reasons why it's just not a good time for them. If this book was entitled "Side Slickology", I would focus on women and the Side Slicks (men) in their lives.

But since the focus of this book is on Side Chickology, I am *focusing* my attention on how men fall prey to extra-marital affairs. From my 30 years of experience in working with couples, what I've found is that men usually have different, what I call "sexpectations" than women have. Men tend to *feel* a much more intense level of disappointment when those sexpectations are not met.

When a man is at the point of frustration due to feelings of sexual deprivation in his marriage, there are a few things that typically cross his mind in no particular order. 1) He contemplates going to a "massage" establishment that provides "happy endings". 2) If he's traveling and away from the house, he may consider hiring a prostitute or private escort to fulfill his sexual fantasies. 3) He considers going to a strip club and possibly getting a lap dance to fulfill his quest for sexual attention. 4) He looks at and masturbates to pornography. 5) He considers a one night stand, or an ongoing, full-blown sexual relationship with someone other than his wife.

Now there's a considerable amount that can be written about each of those five options, but for the sake of focus, I'll limit my comments to options 4 and 5.

PORNOGRAPHY

From a 2013 survey reported by Today.com, 75% of men *admitted* to spending time alone watching pornography.[3] And one of the contributors to this very high percentage of behavior that often includes masturbation or "solo sex" is the inconsistent sexual intimacy in their marriages.

The math is simple – when a man is not getting regular sexual fulfillment from his wife, he literally takes matters into his own hands and pleasures himself.

Now one of the ironies that I've found in so many marriages is the fact that although regular sexual activity was understood to be a part of the union when the decision to marry took place, yet many couples are surprisingly practicing marital celibacy and live in a "sexless marriage". In fact, according to a 2017 Huffington Post article, "Therapists define a sexless relationship as one in which the couple is physically intimate <u>less than 10 times a year</u>."[4] So if those experts are right, then once a month, is very close to being insufficient for a healthy marriage.

So, pornography has become the "go-to" play for both men and women in sexually disappointing marriages. And although pornography may be legal for adults and it may be popular, one thing's for sure, it is far from safe. The statistics are staggering:

The financial cost to business productivity due to pornography use in the U.S. alone is estimated at $16.9 billion annually.

- Every second 28,258 users are watching pornography on the internet

- Every second $3,075.64 is being spent on pornography on the internet

- Every second 372 people are typing the word "adult" into search engines

- 40 million American people regularly visit porn sites

- 35% of all internet downloads are related to pornography

- 25% of all search engine queries are related to pornography, or about 68 million search queries a day

- One-third of porn viewers are women

- Search engines get 116,000 queries every day related to child pornography

- 34% of internet users have experienced unwanted exposure to pornographic content through ads, pop up ads, misdirected links or emails

- 2.5 billion emails sent or received every day contain porn

- Every 39 minutes a new pornography video is being created in the United States

- About 200,000 Americans are "porn addicts"

FAMILY/MARITAL PORNOGRAPHY STATS

- According to an Organization formerly known as the National Coalition for the Protection of Children & Families, 2010, 47% of families in the United States reported that pornography is a problem in their home.

- ***Pornography use increases the marital infidelity rate by more than 300%.***

- 40% of "sex addicts" lose their spouses, 58% suffer considerable financial losses, and about a third lose their jobs.

- 68% of divorce cases involve one party meeting a new paramour over the internet while 56% involve one party having an "obsessive interest" in pornographic websites.[5]

The numbers don't lie and the statistic that I placed in bold print that says that pornography increases marital infidelity by 300 percent is mind-blowing, especially in light of the fact that these statistics don't necessarily view participating in pornography as an act of infidelity. I tend to disagree with that view because in my opinion pornography is virtual infidelity. In any case the developers of these stats still believe that pornography will eventually lead to acts of infidelity. This is why I often refer to Pornography as a playground sliding board to hell. It's pleasurable, fun and erotically stimulating, but the *bottom* of the slide has consequences and costs that are destroying lives and families.

One of the problems with pornography is the fact that it actually trains a person to have orgasms and sexual pleasure without relationship and commitment. So, the more that behavior is repeated, the more programmed the individual becomes to be disconnected while being sexual.

Emotional disconnection is hard to mask in a marriage because it makes a man, in particular, more prone to objectify his wife. It causes her to lose her treasured place of value in his eyes, mind, and heart, because pornography has a way of poisoning our thinking and making us feel entitled to sexual pleasure on demand. That's what pornography is - sexual pleasure on demand.

Any size, color, or position you want with as much frequency as you want, at any time of the day or night that you want it. You don't have to be loving, caring, supportive, communicative, financially responsible, or provide any other basic relational expectation. You don't have to converse on Levels 1, 2, 3, 4, 5, or 6. You don't have to say a word. You can have what you want virtually, any way and anytime you want it. No matter how bad things may be in the reality of your marriage, in the man cave, you are the man!

Meanwhile, under the same roof is the woman you made a marital vow to for the rest of your life, and she's not interested in sex without love, trust, commitment, responsibility, and caring. Therefore, the intimacy gap widens because you have found a way to self-comfort, and now you don't *have* to work on the relationship to restore intimacy, because you've got a substitute – some virtual Side Chicks; and their availability is limitless.

Meanwhile, the marriage doesn't just suffer from a lack of physical intimacy, but emotional intimacy begins to fade. Because when a man is internally conflicted by his secret obsession with porn, he will often begin to justify his behavior in his own mind by vilifying his wife. "She's no fun," he thinks to himself. "The kids are more important to her; they're her world."

Additionally, when a married couple isn't close, oftentimes, cynical thoughts about each other become a regular part of their private thinking. "He's so selfish and unkind," she thinks. "She spends money like we're wealthy with no regard to budgeting and saving," he surmises. These un-expressed, yet deeply felt, and regularly thought sentiments about each other create a greater wedge between the couple.

These are the same people who once loved each other so much that during their wedding ceremony, the traditional marital vows read by the minister weren't enough. They wrote their own love-ridden odes to one another, expressing how "just meeting each other" has changed their world for good forever. Now they've gotten to a point where they can't be in each other's presence without feeling hurt and anger.

So, she dives into books, Pilates, her nails, and the kids, and he dives into work, his car, ESPN and his man cave. Unfortunately, what happens in the man cave doesn't always *stay* in the man cave.

WHEN VIRTUAL IS NO LONGER ENOUGH

In Old Testament literature, there's a phrase that says, "The eye is not satisfied with seeing."[6] The truth is, whatever we gaze at long enough can very easily move from fantasy to desire. When a man feeds his mind with thousands of sexually explicit images that he pleasures himself to, over time he will view women through a lens of lust that makes him see them as potential conquests.

Although a man can be hooked on virtual sex for decades, many times his sexual appetite becomes so ravenous from all of the non-relational, pleasure-only sex, that virtual is no longer enough. Now he's craving the "real thing", because the eye is never satisfied with just seeing, and this is not new.

Around 1,000 B.C., David was the King of Israel. He ascended the ladder of success amazingly, moving from a non-aristocratic family into a military hero and eventually the most powerful man of his day.

One day, while David was scheduled to be leading his troops in war, he chose instead to stay home in his palace. That afternoon, following a nap, David went to what may have been *his* man cave, up on the roof of his palace. As he strolled along the roof, he noticed a woman at a nearby home, bathing herself in the outer courtyard of her home.

Now it's easy to assume indiscretion on the woman's part, however, she was actually still within the privacy and confines of her living quarters and not open to the public eye. It just so happens that David was able to see her because of the elevation level of the roof of his palace.

When David saw this nude woman bathing herself named Bathsheba (no pun intended), he didn't change the channel, or shut down his computer, he enjoyed every moment of it. He fantasized in his mind what it would be like to be with her and probably thought about how hard he'd worked for his nation and his family, and how he deserved to have a good time. (Entitlement is one of the biggest motivators for people to cross the line and commit sexually immoral acts.)

So, there's David, who called into work and took the day off, standing on his roof being a voyeur, and every time the suds and water would give way to Bathsheba's beautiful anatomy, the more aroused David became until he couldn't resist anymore. His eye was not satisfied with just seeing.

With his heart pounding and his adrenaline levels elevated, he called for his staff to inform him regarding who the woman was that had caught his eye. In spite of the fact that he learned that her name was Bathsheba and that she was the wife of another man named Uriah, David was already at the point of no return. He commanded the naked woman to be brought to him immediately, and the King used his power to force himself on this woman sexually. The eye is not satisfied with seeing.

And if you want to see the chaos and consequences that this act of uncontrolled passion caused in David's life and the lives of many others, just read the story in 2 Samuel chapters 11 through 18. It's a very sobering account.

In summary, the woman was impregnated by David, David had her husband killed to protect himself from retaliation, she was swiftly married to David to cover everything up, and the baby that was born from this union died. If that weren't enough, subsequently, one of David's daughters (Tamar) was raped by one of his sons (Amnon), just like David forced himself on Bathsheba. In retaliation for Tamar's raping, one of David's other sons, Absalom, killed Amnon for raping his sister Tamar. Then Absalom started a revolt against his father's throne, and attempted to kill his own father, but he was killed by one of David's soldiers.

So, an innocent man (Uriah) was killed, two women were sexually assaulted and left with the emotional scars for the rest of their lives, and David lost three sons following this decision to cross the line.

All of that death, bloodshed, violence, rape, and deceit followed one afternoon of uncontrolled passion fed by just looking at a nude woman who was somebody else's wife. That was pornography in antiquity.

Pornography is a virtual form of infidelity that can lead to a real form of infidelity because the eye is not satisfied with just seeing. Eventually the porn site history of viewing *unknown* women will evolve into the cell phone call and text history of *known* women. Pornography is a sliding board to hell, and the playground where it's housed is right in the man cave.

I heard someone say recently that the key to resisting temptation is to value what the temptation is putting at risk. That's a profound statement, one that we should keep in mind, especially when our marriages are less than pleasurable and satisfying. If we don't, we may end up making a bad situation far worse because of poor decisions.

In fact, ask yourself the question right now: What is being put at risk by the thing that I am being tempted to do? And what will resisting this temptation protect that is of value in my life? My marriage? My career? My reputation? My family? My home? My ministry? My professional practice?

We live in a world that has made a god out of happiness. Whatever makes us happy, we're committed to it, whether it's good or bad. Yet, when given a choice, it's best to choose legacy over pleasure.

BOYFRIEND VS. HUSBAND MENTALITY

Along that same vein, men in general, especially single men who have children, need to step up to the plate and stop living the "Boyfriend Life" and living with a "Boyfriend Mentality" and go all in and be a committed husband and family man. God didn't give Adam a wife until he was a responsible man. A lot of single men don't want to be husbands because being a boy is more fun. It's like being in high school all over again and every weekend has the potential to be like prom night. He knows that a wife would make him focus and hold him accountable, so to keep his liberty he chooses to be "friends with benefits". Why get married and mess up all the fun?

Many women are frustrated and discouraged today because they keep running into and interacting with men who'd rather continue to be boys when it comes to commitment and marriage. Real men make commitments. Boys play games, that's why they're called "players". In fact, that self-centered immaturity is celebrated and lauded amongst other immature, self-centered men as having "game". He's got game because he's got dames. As long as he can get the sexual benefits of marriage without the commitment of marriage, he'll continue to be a boyfriend. Many of you ladies are disappointed in his unwillingness to step up and mature. But you keep having sex with him like he's your husband, you cook for him, like he's your husband, you live with him, like he's your husband, and you're having his babies, like he's your husband. So, while he's playing games like a high school boyfriend, you're playing house like an elementary school girl, satisfied with fantasizing like you're married. Remember how we used to play house as children? Someone would act like the wife, and someone else would act like the husband, but it was all make-believe? So, check this out. He's still playing something called game, and you're still playing something called house, and both of you need to wake up and grow up.

Men, how much better would you be generationally if you were married? (It's different for you than for single women. You have options.) *How much better off would your children or step-children and grandchildren, step-grandchildren, adoptive children, etc. be if you were all in and not single?*

When you die, would you rather be known as a Player or a Patriarch?

Now every single man is not a player. That would be an overstatement. However, if you're single primarily because you don't want to give up the fun you have being "free", then I'm asking you: Is God CALLING you to a higher, more selfless assignment? Particularly marriage and fathering?

Life and marriage are full of forks in the road, where we are brought to decisions between what might make us *happy* and what would be *best* for our family and legacy. Choose long-term legacy over short-term happiness

Unfortunately, many people are driven by the phrase in the Declaration of Independence that offers life, liberty, and the pursuit of happiness. So, we end up leaving our marriages because we want to be happy. Oftentimes, we leave because we've already gotten inappropriately close to someone *outside* of our marriage that makes us happy.

But as we'll see in Chapters 7 and 8, if you play that video all the way out into a blended family, baby mama drama, custody cases, step-children, awkward holiday moments, expensive legal fees, disrupted family trees, inheritance confusion, and on and on and on, sometimes the *cost* of happiness is higher than we anticipated.

Conversely, the *value* of legacy continues to pay dividends for generations. It gives hope to your children and their children, that lasting marriages are possible in spite of the ever-growing number of marriages ending in divorce. It strengthens family solidarity and unity. Legacy choices are worth the sacrifice.

On the other hand, we must beware of a word that describes the space between happiness and legacy, and that word is *compromise*. Whenever we have to philosophically justify our actions and decisions, it's probably because we're choosing happiness and pleasure over legacy.

I've heard people say about their decision to end their marital commitment to pursue a life of fun for themselves, "Keith, I'm ready to just do me." In other words, "I want to do what makes me happy, period."

But here's a prayer that I recommend that we all pray for the safety of our families and our legacies, "Lord, help me to do what's right and not just do me."

Affirmations

I will seek genuine intimacy and connection with my spouse instead of seeking virtual pleasure with strangers.

I will read books, watch videos, go to counseling, and do whatever else is necessary to strengthen my ability to communicate effectively with my spouse.

CHAPTER 3:

A GIRLFRIEND MENTALITY
(THE MAKING OF A SIDE CHICK)

I think being a Side Chick begins with the way a woman views herself. Too often women have been content viewing themselves as a girlfriend. It's a status that they value. That's ok when you're a teenager, but if at some point, you don't have a shift in your thinking from being girlfriend material to being wife material, you will always have a "girlfriend mentality", which will impact what you expect and accept in your life relationally.

It's interesting that in the Old Testament Book of Proverbs we're told that, "*He who finds a wife finds what is good and receives favor from the Lord.*"[1]

This verse has been debated lately from an interpretive stand point. There are those who subscribe to the position that the "woman" referred to in this verse as "a wife that a man finds" was described as a "wife" when the man first "found" or met her. This is not to suggest that she was already married to someone else, but that she was prepared to be a wife before someone took her hand in marriage.

Others debate that from a hermeneutic standpoint, the word "good" in the verse should precede the word "wife" in the verse and thus good is the description of the type of woman the man ends up marrying. In other words, when a man finds or actually *marries* a good wife as opposed to a less than good wife, then he receives favor from the Lord. Therefore, the emphasis should be placed on the kind of wife the man ends up with instead of assuming that she was a prepared wife when he first met her.

Although I can see merit in both arguments, the challenge for me comes in the second clause of the verse that says that this man, "receives favor from the Lord." My question is, at what point does he receive favor from the Lord? When he "finds" a wife or a good wife? Or when he marries her and discovers that she's good?

The reality is, no matter how you interpret that very interesting verse of scripture, some women are more prepared for the role of wife than others because of their development and disposition. I'm convinced that this verse is describing the woman that a man finds to marry as a "wife" before she's even married. She's single, but she's wife material. She's unmarried, but she has all of the qualities and attributes and character of a faithful wife. When a man "finds" her, he has found something good *and* he receives favor from the Lord.

Certainly, it is not beyond the realm of possibility to believe that God can prepare a woman to be a wife *before* she is married. Indeed, the first man recorded in human history, Adam, was placed in a deep sleep by God, and when he awoke, he was presented with a wife, not a girlfriend named Eve.[2] Whatever she needed to be a wife, those things were in place when Adam first laid eyes on her.

My life and experience tell me that some women have a wifely disposition even while they are single, while others don't always think and operate that way.

So, the question is, if you're a woman reading this book and you're single, are you a wife in your mindset, or are you mentally a girlfriend? What's the difference?

WIFE VS. GIRLFRIEND THINKING

A girlfriend mentality is when you're content being *an important part* of a man's life, rather than being his most important human priority.

Another distinction is the fact that the typical mindset of a wife is that she only has sex with her *husband*. If you're single and not celibate, that means you're thinking and operating like a girlfriend and a man is getting husband-level benefits from you, when he's only made a boyfriend-level commitment to you. Moreover, some men are getting husband-level benefits from you that haven't even made a public-courtship-level commitment to you. That makes you a chick in the closet or a "Hide Chick". An unmarried man that's hiding his connection to you on a dating level, is not about to go public with you as a wife. He doesn't view you as someone worthy enough to reveal his relationship with you. So, you end up settling for being intimate in the night, but a stranger in the light.

By contrast, when you have a wife's mentality, even as a single woman, you require that any serious courtship relationship that a man has with you be a public thing. He must meet your family and close friends and perhaps even ask for your father's blessing to court you and certainly get his permission to eventually marry you. That way the relationship is out in the open. This protects you from manipulative men who prey on women who are not ensconced in a circle of support and love in their lives.

This is a very critical distinction right here because the reality is, so many of these secret relationships that operate behind a veil of privacy because one or both members of the couple ascribe to the philosophy that "we don't want people in our business", is leading people into unaccountable abysses of shame and hurt. In fact, even private marriage ceremonies are dangerous in my opinion. First of all, why would you make some of the most sacred vows, and one of the most important decisions and covenants you can make with another person, and not have all of the people who have loved you and cared for you all of your life to not only be a part of the ceremony, but to also be a part of the approval process? That's dangerous.

More often than not, the woman ends up with the short end of the stick. Sadly, women with girlfriend mentalities will take *any* ceremony that elevates their status on paper with a man, even if no one is allowed to know that it ever happened. That's ridiculous.

There's a reason why traditional marital vows include the statement, "Who gives this woman to be married to this man?" That statement is read because it's understood that this woman has been nurtured and protected by another male and/or female authority up until this point, and that her husband to be has been researched and approved by that authority before he's allowed to change her last name to his last name.

What is even more dangerous and vulnerable than the woman who gets married to a man without anyone's knowledge, is the woman that is intimately involved with a man on a sexual level and hasn't even had a private wedding. She's in a relationship with a man that hasn't made any legal commitment to her. She's just an undercover lover. Only women with a girlfriend mindset will allow that kind of relationship because they believe that something beats nothing.

Although the philosophy that something beats nothing is true in the world of numbers, it's not true if the something is manipulation, being used, getting sexually transmitted diseases, having unplanned and unwanted pregnancies, not knowing what your future holds, and investing your all into *something and someone* that won't give you a return on your investment. In my humble opinion, "nothing" beats *that* every single day!

Now I'm sure that what I'm expressing here may sound very old-fashioned, maybe even anachronous. Some of you may even feel my tone and position here is condescending and insensitive and I certainly don't intend to come across that way. The truth is, because I listen to and see so many devastated and hurting women who find themselves almost inconsolable because of these very matters, I'm not only waving a red flag, but I'm trying my best to provide an alternative route to escape this very painful road that so many are headed down.

If you're a single woman, I'm not suggesting that you never date. Courtship is critical in giving you enough time to discover whom the person that you're involved with *really* is. In fact, you need an extended period of courtship to see who they are behind the scenes and off the record. How do they manage their money? How do they get along with their family and friends? How do they work and where do they work? What are their true desires and interests? What are their goals and values regarding the future, raising children, education, family, faith, etc.? Courtship is a must!

FRIENDS WITH BENEFITS

It seems that one of the "benefits" of moving from just being acquaintances to being "steady friends" is the fact that most people make that the phase of the relationship where eventually sexual intercourse is introduced.

Now that we "go together" or "we're a couple", (unless someone has made it clear from the outset that they're practicing celibacy until marriage), the dating stage is the stage where sex is almost expected. That's a huge mistake. In fact, celibacy is critical! Celibacy, during courtship, gives us clarity in the relationship, while copulation at this stage leads to ambiguity.

The reason for the mental confusion that's caused by a non-marital sexual relationship is because sexual intercourse is such a deeply personal, profound, and sacred thing, when you introduce it into the wrong environment, which is any non-marital environment, it clouds your thinking. Because now, I'm not just dealing with a boyfriend or girlfriend, I'm dealing with "my lover... we've been intimate." *That,* my friends, is a game changer!

Now everything gets cloudy. Now the relationship is focused on an area that was supposed to be reserved for husbands and wives, and because so much focus is now on the quality and frequency of the sex, the other more important things that need to be discovered, remain a mystery.

So now the two of you are regularly having sex, but in spite of the fact that you've opened your legs, he still hasn't opened up to you about some things in his past that remain a mystery.

Because there is an unseen but genuine connection between a woman's vagina and her heart, whenever she lets a man enter her vagina it's only because she's allowed him to enter her heart.

Men, on the other hand, tend to be more dis-integrated sexually, primarily because we are taught from the time that we were boys to shut down our emotions and ignore our feelings.

One day, I was having lunch with author and psychotherapist Richard Cohen and he shared with me that, "We were wrongly taught as little boys to, 'man up, and stop acting like a little girl,' whenever we were hurt emotionally and expressed that pain with crying and tears. So, over the course of time, we gradually learned how to shut down our souls, and we ultimately became unresponsive emotionally from the front of our shoulders to our waists, which is our emotional core region. So, the only connection that we have to our genitalia (below our waists) is our heads (above our shoulders). And the primary motivator for us sexually is our eyes. So, our eyes communicate to our private area something desirable and we go after it without emotion. That's why one of the greatest healing experiences a man could ever have is to get reacquainted with his feelings and understand what's going on inside of himself internally."[3]

This is very important to understand ladies, because when dating includes sex, essentially you often find yourself in a classic negotiation of compromise as you give your body in the hopeful exchange for love and commitment. Unfortunately, more often than not it backfires. You think, "Maybe if I give him 'some', then he'll see how serious I am about this relationship and he'll take the relationship to the next level, marriage."

But in actuality, your chastity as a woman could be the one last precious thing about you that will make him long to marry you, but if he gets "it" for "free", then he's prone to not pay the full price for it later.

I could go on and on talking about the detriment and consequences of pre-marital sex, but what I want to emphasize instead is the powerful benefits of celibacy during courtship.

When the relationship is free from sexual activity, celibacy helps a man to truly make a decision regarding you. I've seen it over and over again with couples that I've worked with. A non-sexual courtship helps a man to come to a decision swiftly about you as a woman. This is because any man that can't have sex with you while the two of you are dating will eventually either move on, or he'll step up to the plate, really get to know you, and maybe even eventually marry you.

Contrarily, please pardon the antiquated expression, but any man that's getting the milk without buying the cow, will live in indecision for years, if not decades.

There's no need to decide because he's getting marital-level benefits from you without making a marital-level commitment to you. However, when you choose to be celibate, watch how men will make much swifter decisions concerning you to either leave you alone or to make you their focus and ultimately their bride. Ladies, your decision to be celibate could save you *years* of being on hold in a relationship, not knowing when or where it's going.

Let me be clear ladies; when you make the celibacy decision, you'll have to go through your share of hurt and rejection. But it's better to be hurt by a man that didn't get what he was really there for (sex), than to be hurt by a man who got it and still didn't give you what you wanted, which was his allegiance and commitment to you forever.

I cannot emphasize enough how important celibacy is. Even if you're engaged to someone, if you're having sex as a single woman with the man you're going to marry, that can still have damaging effects on the marriage relationship because pre-marital sexual activity impacts future marital fidelity. In fact, sexual activity in dating is often the root that eventually leads to the fruit of infidelity in marriage. The scriptures say, "*Don't be misled—you cannot mock the justice of God. You will always harvest what you plant.*"[4]

Marriage is the fence around sex to protect it and keep it in its proper context. However, if we don't respect the fence enough to stay *outside* of it *before* marriage, we may not respect the fence enough to stay *inside* of it *after* marriage. This is why sexual activity in dating literally trains us towards infidelity in marriage. (This book is primarily about Marriage, but I spend an extended amount of time telling Single People 8 things you need to do and to know as a single in Chapter 10.)

But celibacy is not the only thing that will help to keep you from being a life-long girlfriend, there's another thing you must not do. In addition to not having pre-marital sex, you shouldn't be supporting your boyfriend financially. That's not your responsibility as a girlfriend. That's a mother or a wife's job. (One you should never be to him and the other you may or may not become to him.) Stop paying his bills. If you are helping your boyfriend pay his bills, then you're a girlfriend, doing wife-level service to a person that hasn't made a husband-level commitment to you.

Before I ask any more questions about your being a "girlfriend", my question to you is simply, why do you do it? Why are you *acting* like a wife, when you have girlfriend status? That's a girlfriend mentality at work.

I think there are a lot of women who are actually hurting their chances to be the wife that they desire to be because they keep settling for being a girlfriend by title, but a wife in every other aspect for a man. But the reality is, a lifetime girlfriend will rarely become a full-time wife.

You must carry yourself like a wife before you get married, because when a man is ready to get married, he's not looking for another girlfriend, he's searching for a wife.

Perhaps a lady reading that will think, "Well how will he know that I can provide those things for him as a wife if I don't show him as his girlfriend?" That's a great question and it stands to reason that if a woman practices celibacy, then he may very well not know how "good she is in the bed" as the saying goes or how compatible they are sexually. If she doesn't support a man financially that's she's not married to, he may not get a feel for how supportive she is.

But here's what you have to understand. When a man finds a woman that he wants to spend the rest of his life with, he has fallen in love with so much more than her body and her pocketbook. He loves her on so many different levels mentally, emotionally, spiritually, psychologically, platonically, etc. that if she's great in bed and financially supportive that's all a bonus!

So don't worry about proving yourself in those areas during courtship, because doing that will cloud the relationship and prevent him from discovering all of the other things that are great about you.

Affirmations

While dating, I will choose celibacy and clarity
over sexual activity and ambiguity.

I will not give a man wife-level support
and benefits who's only made
a boyfriend-level or less commitment to me.

CHAPTER 4:

THE PRELUDE TO SIDE CHICK STATUS

Before a person moves into an active state of infidelity, typically they have to figure out a way to justify the inappropriate behavior within their own conscience. According to VeryWellMind.com "Psychologist Leon Festinger proposed the theory of cognitive dissonance centered on how people try to reach internal consistency. He suggested that people have an inner need to ensure that their beliefs and behaviors are consistent. That is because inconsistent or conflicting beliefs lead to disharmony, which people strive to avoid."[1]

When a person knows that they're engaged in something that is in conflict with their beliefs and values, either they have to stop the behavior to eliminate the internal civil war, or they have to somehow convince themselves that what they are doing is not *that* bad.

I hold the belief that any sexual relationship that occurs between a married man or woman with anyone other than their spouse is a violation of the marital covenant of fidelity and is therefore wrong. Most of the men that I have talked to over the years would agree that "stepping out on their wives" is a clear violation. Whenever they are contemplating acting out that kind of behavior, there is something inside of them that says, "That's not right... Don't cross that line." There is always an internal uneasiness about the whole thing.

So, in order for a man to *justify* proceeding in his efforts to engage in an inappropriate relationship outside of his marriage, he typically doesn't try to convince himself that *bad* (adultery) is *good*. Instead, he works hard to convince himself psychologically that *bad* (adultery) is "not *so* bad when it's consenting adults." "And, at least I'm not out here killing anybody" he tells himself. "I work hard, and I treat everyone fairly. I'm not a bank robber. I'm not a pedophile. I'm not a rapist. I just have someone that I've gotten really close to that I enjoy spending time with, and I have a lot of chemistry with. But we both respect our spouses and families, and we would never try to hurt either of them." You see how that works?

He's created just enough wiggle room to rationalize functioning in an affair. Now the "game" begins.

TENNIS ANYONE?

Any man that's going to cross the line and violate his marital covenant must practice what is called in certain street vernacular "game". By game I mean strategic flirtation with a specific goal in mind, and it starts with what the world of Sexual Addiction Therapy refers to as "Grooming".

Grooming is often done by Sexual Predators on unsuspecting children. The predator befriends the child with gifts and favors to minimize the boundaries between the adult and the child, making them more vulnerable to sexual abuse.

When it comes to adults, it's usually not abuse that's the intended goal, rather a consenting sexual relationship. Nevertheless, the "predator" still has to orchestrate circumstances and conversations in such a way to discover whether or not the other person is open to and interested in the same thing.

Years ago, I heard Pastor Tommy Nelson of Denton Bible Church in Denton, Texas describe this stage of flirtation as analogous to a tennis match. Certainly, it's not always the man, that's the aggressor, sometimes it's the woman, but for the purpose of this analogy, we'll make the man the aggressor/server.

Initially, the man will spend days or weeks thinking in his mind of a statement that he can make to this particular person that he knows or has periodic interactions with, that is forward enough to be interpreted as a flirtatious "pass" at the woman, but neutral enough to be refuted as a misunderstanding if she doesn't go for the bait. This calculated statement is very powerful because he has thought for weeks about how it will all unfold, how he will dodge the moment and escape if she gets upset or offended by it, and how he will smile in relief and with a feeling of success if she embraces the statement favorably.

He'll "serve" his statement like a tennis player, and wait to see if and how the serve is "returned". His calculated serve might be, "I wish my wife would listen to me the way that you do, Sandy. I just want to be heard. Your husband is one lucky man." Then there's that nail biting moment of silence as he awaits her "return".

She responds sheepishly, "Ray, that's so kind of you. You always say the nicest things. I'm so sorry that your wife doesn't listen to you. You're so easy to talk to. Unfortunately, my 'husband', if that's what you want to call him, doesn't say two words to me in a day. He's too busy playing golf and hanging out with his buddies to even converse with me. But thanks for the compliment." And ladies and gentlemen, Ray has scored an ace in his journey towards adultery.

Because he has prepared himself for weeks or even months for this moment, he's already prepared to score more points in this "match". So he says with all the sincerity he can muster, "You've *gotta* be kidding me Sandy. You are married to a man that won't talk to you!? I could talk to you all day." (Another smooth serve.)

Her return, "Yup, it's true. Our communication is terrible. Outside of a few passing words about the kids or our schedules, we say very little to each other, and I hate it."

He volleys, "I know exactly how you feel." And since Ray knows that he's made significant progress towards his goal he relaxes the game by saying, "Let's talk about something positive. How's that project you've been working on?"

Now the irony of Ray's concern for Sandy is the fact that he hasn't asked his wife about her day or her work or goals in years. Because Ray has some inside information on how bad the communication is in

Sandy's marriage, when they have subsequent conversations over the next several days, every time he sees or talks to Sandy, he will begin the conversation with the question, "Are things any better at home communication-wise?" He's asking because he's hoping that things are the same, so that Sandy can be reminded of how bad things are in her home, while experiencing so much fun when talking to him.

Now because Ray, is interested in this "relationship" going to another level, after much thought, he'll come up with another killer serve.

PITY PARTY INVITATION

Ray's next move/serve is to pull on Sandy's heart-string by getting her to feel sorry for him. While they're on the phone, he will intentionally make sure he sounds like he's in a very low place emotionally. He'll make sure that Sandy hears deep dejection in his voice to the point where she asks him, "Ray, what's wrong? You seem very sad."

His response, "It's what's been wrong for the last four years of my marriage." (Here comes the exaggeration). "Sandy, forgive me if I'm being too personal, but I'm just going to be real with you. Bev and I have only been intimate three times in the last four years." (Now this shift in conversation is significant and strategic because Ray's hope is, if Sandy has been open and helpful in meeting his communication needs, maybe she'd be willing to meet his sexual needs as well.)

Ray continues, "And I know marriage is not all about sex, but as a man, I just feel like less than once a year is unreasonable!" (Of course, three times in the last four years is unreasonable. That's why he didn't tell Sandy the truth, that they have actually been having sex about once or twice a month for the last 4 years, which is not a lot in the opinion of some, but not nearly as bad.)

Sandy's volley/return, "First of all, Ray, I'm *so* sorry that you're going through that in your marriage. And you don't have to apologize to me for being honest. I want you to be honest with me. That doesn't bother me at all." Then Sandy asks, "Has she given you a reason why she's not interested in sex?"

Ray's volley, "Yeah, she says she doesn't *feel* sexy, and it hinders her from getting in the mood. So, I'm like, 'well what am I supposed to do?' And then she just shuts down, and we'll go months without even talking about it." "Listen Sandy", Ray continues, "I don't want to drag you into my personal mess and I don't want to paint my wife as a bad person. She really isn't. I love her. I love my family, and I'm committed to them. But she's making this so hard for me.

I just wish I had someone who understood what I was going through… (slight pause to increase empathy and to put a little English on the serve). I feel like I'm being punished and tormented and I'm just tired. I know it's wrong and please don't judge me, I just hate feeling like I'm a burden to my wife. But at the same time I have needs as a man. You know what I mean? Does that make sense?"

Sandy's return, "It makes perfect sense…" Followed by deafening silence, which is Sandy giving him a lob return that he can slam. Her succinct statement implies not just understanding and agreement, but empathy, compassion, and "I'm ready for you to lead us to the next steps."

Meanwhile, it's a silence that Ray is optimistic about but not sure how to interpret, so to act as if he's unaware of the silence, he strategically and deceitfully breaks the silence by faking like he temporarily lost a cell phone signal when he says, "Sandy? Can you hear me?"

She says, "Yes, I can hear you."

He responds, "Oh, ok, I lost you for a second there." Which makes her repeat her earlier response, "I'm not sure if you heard me, but I said what you're saying makes perfect sense and your honesty doesn't offend me. In fact, it's kind of funny how we both have spouses that won't talk to us and are starving us sexually." Game, set, match!

All Ray needs to do now is to keep the serve and volley going, and it's just a matter of time and place before he and Sandy cross the line and the rest will be history.

Now in the scenario that I just described, both persons are married. However, oftentimes, the Side Chick is single, and there are some important things to highlight about a single Side Chick.

HISTORY'S FIRST SIDE CHICK

In the Old Testament Book of Genesis in the 16th chapter, we're told that after years and years of unsuccessfully trying to have children, Sarai suggested to her husband Abram that he have a sexual relationship with her maidservant Hagar, with the hopes that "perhaps I (Sarai) can build a family through her (Hagar)."[2]

Abram agreed to this arrangement (without hesitation I might add) and the woman who was previously Sarai's servant, became Abram's concubine. Now Abram has a "wife-approved, live-in Side Chick." Unbelievable.

And believe it or not, it seems as though this "arrangement" was progressing fairly well until the plan actually worked and backfired at the same time. For just as Sarai wanted, Abram "slept with Hagar and she conceived. (The only problem is) when she (Hagar) knew she was pregnant, she began to despise her mistress (Sarai)."[3]

Now before she got into a sexual relationship with Abram, there is no record of any tension between Hagar and Sarai. But once she became for Abram what Sarai was unable to be, (the mother of his own child), she began to disrespect his wife Sarai.

Usually, Side Chicks have a level of disrespect for the wives of the husbands that they're intimately involved with and part of the reason for that is the fact that the Side Chick is aware of the wife's shortcomings in areas where the Side Chick has strengths. In this case, Sarai's deficiency, her infertility; was Hagar's strength, her fertility.

Sometimes the flaws of the wife are revealed to the Side Chick by the husband in order to get enough empathy from the Side Chick to comfort him with a sexual relationship.

That's a double betrayal. To have sex with another woman is betrayal, but in addition to that to divulge personal deficiencies about your wife is another betrayal altogether. This understandably causes an even deeper gash in the betrayed wife's soul. Unfortunately, it's all a part of the "game" in Side Chickology.

Meanwhile, the Side Chick uses the negative information about the "less than sufficient" wife to justify her stepping in to support this mistreated, under-nurtured, pitiful man. She's a "good Samaritan".

I don't mean to over-state this scenario or to understate the fact that some marriages are downright lonely, empty, sexless, and hopeless, and are primed and ready for infidelity. (Remember, I am addressing this very complicated and multi-faceted subject with a very broad brush.) But the reality is, once there is someone else in the picture that is meeting spouse-level needs, then the person receiving those forbidden, extra-marital benefits is a lot less interested in and motivated to work on their marriage. In those cases, the limited attention is less frustrating at home, when there's greater attention outside of the home.

There's something very important that we can learn from history's first Side Chick, and that is the fact that Side Chicks are gap fillers. They fill in where there is a lack or a breach. She'll do what the wife is either unable or unwilling to do for her husband.

She'll study a man until she discovers what he's missing and all she needs to do is provide what he's missing and she then becomes a focal point for him because she is now filling a gap in his life. If the husband has some sort of insatiable appetite that the wife can't realistically feed, the side-chick will be his "seconds" to fill up on when the meals at home aren't satisfying his ravenous penchant.

She'll study what he likes by way of hobbies or special gifts, and she'll make sure he gets what he likes. She'll make sure that she understands what pleasures him sexually, and she'll make sure that he gets what he wants. If there are certain things about his wife that annoys him, the Side Chick will conscientiously avoid doing or saying those things that will annoy or upset him. She becomes the epitome of everything he desires in a woman; the perfect high.

This is what makes the side chick relationship so addictive and irresistible. It's like an amusement park of pleasure on demand for a man, that's impossible for a wife with children and all of the responsibilities of real life to compete with.

THE BUILD UP

Back to Sandy and Ray. When we left them, they were connecting conversationally over the fact that they both were communication and sex-starved spouses in bad marriages. So, what happens next?

Typically, there's still a process that leads to a literal sexual affair because there's still a lot at stake so both persons have to be fastidious about it. Now that the emotional line of fidelity has been crossed and Ray and Sandy are into each other, there's a more concerted effort to keep the nature of their relationship undetected.

They begin to protect their cell phones from discovery. They may even change the way the other person's name appears on their phone, giving them alternative names to protect their identity from their spouses especially, because the calls and texts become more frequent and they happen at late hours and during commutes and at times when they are not around their spouse.

Now that they've already gotten past the first level of flirting which is the precaution phase where very calculated risks are taken to see if there's mutual interest, the second level of flirting usually shifts towards jest and subtle humor, to keep things progressing safely.

During a conversation where they're experiencing their normal laughter and amusement, Ray pulls out his killer serve and says chuckling, "Sandy, I was just thinking, as sexless as your marriage is, you're probably hornier than I am!" And they both burst into laughter.

If Sandy wants to continue to enjoy the obvious chase from Ray she might simply say while laughing, "You're probably right." Or if she wants to send him back a lob return that he can easily slam, she might say, "I guess you'll have to find out." Now if that last statement was sent via text, it would also include an emoji wink face and smile.

So now the relationship has accelerated to the door of physical infidelity and it's only a matter of time before everything is set up for execution.

Now all of the conversations are much more intimate and sensual and they shift from just cell phone texts to emails and private direct messages on various social media platforms to further protect the relationship from exposure.

Things then progress to virtual sexual activity as requests are made, usually by the visually-stimulated man, for sensual bathing-suit pictures, and eventually photos of nude body parts are shared. Nude Face Time conversations that may include masturbation is next, and of course plans for the "Grand Slam" are made.

"When can we get together?" Ray asks. "You tell me, I can't wait," Sandy replies.

Many of you reading this chapter can relate to what I've described. For some, you may be experiencing this right now! I warn you, if you're "Ray" or "Sandy" in this story right now, the cost of this affair will be a price you don't want to pay. The damage that it will do to so many people is incalculable as we'll see in Chapters 6 & 7. Please cease and desist.

Affirmations

I will acknowledge my attempts to groom and resist the urge to flirt by avoiding people and environments that feed those behaviors.

I will create, respect, and honor protective marital boundaries for the sake of my family, reputation, career, and future.

CHAPTER 5:

THE RUSH OF SECRECY

Who can forget the emotional excitement that we had as children when we played games like hide-and-go-seek? The internal rush of energy we felt then as adolescents may have been our first real "high" in life. The thrill of utilizing our deceptive prowess to avoid detection and the heart-palpitating buzz that we felt as we secluded ourselves in a hiding spot that no one could discover us gave us a feeling of both invigoration and accomplishment.

Whenever you shared a hiding spot with a fellow player in the game of hide-and-go-seek, you both felt connected on some level and you both felt like you were collectively smarter than anyone else playing the game. Usually, there was a leader amongst the two of you when hiding, but in order to be successful, there had to be mutual collaboration. Thus, we learned very early in life, that effective hiding can feel like winning.

When a person is engaged in an affair, even at the pre-sexual intercourse level, the adrenaline rush that they get from this new, hidden, secretive relationship is almost uncontainable. It blows away anything else going on their lives, and before anyone counts to 10 this "playful" relationship has been hidden and continues to be meticulously hidden sometimes for years.

In fact, the married man in this case starts becoming less and less "available" at home. He may be in the house physically, but emotionally and mentally he's checked out. He's trying to sneak to his phone and laptop every chance he gets to see if the Side Chick has sent him a direct message, text, email or if she tried to call him.

Meanwhile the emotional tension begins to rise in a man's marriage at this point as he starts to get questions and curiosity from his wife, that are fed by both her discernment that something's not right, and/or by data that she either stumbles across or searches for and discovers.

Social media platforms and cell phones usually have all of the incriminating information that's needed to prove inappropriate behavior or activity.

Which is why at this stage the husband becomes very protective of his phone. In fact, he will become irrationally agitated and defensive when his wife asks him about his phone. For example, if she says, "Honey, can I see your phone?" His response will be, "Why? Your phone is right there. Why do you need to see my phone? No, you can't see my phone. Why do you always need to see my phone? Do I ask to see your phone? You're always looking for something. I'm tired of that. I told you a thousand times, there's nothing to see. Get that out of your head, woman. Stop making stuff up about me in your head. (Expletive)." Whenever a man says all of that in response to a request to see his phone, that's a strong suggestion that he's hiding something and he's trying to shut his wife down so she'll stop the search.

Furthermore, when he's hiding inappropriate interactions on his phone, he will never lay it down face up and leave it out in the open. Whenever he places it on a table wherever he may be, he will keep the screen face down, because he never knows when a call or text or message might come from his Side Chick that may raise questions from others, especially his wife.

Infidelity, even at the pre-sexual stage (which makes it an emotional affair at this point), makes men a lot less productive. They deliver less on their jobs and they deliver at a lower level and it's primarily because they're so consumed by this relationship that requires a lot of energy to nurture and keep undisclosed at the same time. Hiding requires a lot of work.

Another thing that starts happening is both the Side Slick (husband) and the Side Chick become really secluded in their lives. In some cases, they even move from being these outgoing people who connect with friends on a regular basis, to suddenly becoming less engaged with even their close friends. And when their friends address their absence and lack of availability, they usually blame it on work or family responsibilities or being swamped with grad school work or some other project. Because they know that their closes friends love them too much to allow them to be in such a dangerous relationship, so they keep this secret very close to their vests.

RUNNING RED LIGHTS AND STOP SIGNS

In the area where I live, there are devices at many major traffic intersections called Red Light Traffic Cameras. And if you aren't familiar with them, you run a red light, and you will be.

In fact, you'll receive a hefty fine in the mail with multiple pictures of your vehicle committing the crime, with close up shots of your license plate so that the evidence is undeniable. I've certainly received my share of those citations in the mail, and they serve as a costly reminder that violating rules will one day catch up with you.

The world of infidelity is slightly different. The "red lights" and "stop signs" are intended to stop us, but when we run through them, we don't always get fined a few days later. The "bill" usually comes further down the road, and the cost is very sizeable.

Many times, when a person is about to jeopardize all that they have worked hard to build by having an extra-marital affair, there will be gracious roadblocks placed in their pathway to try to deter them to choose a better way. I view that as God's divine love and grace at work trying to protect us.

Unfortunately, the rush and passion that is felt towards the other person overrides the warnings, and the people run through the "red lights".

By "red lights", I mean the time when your child walked in the room while you were Face Timing your Side Chick, and you quickly ended the call and pretended as if you were looking at a You Tube video. That was a red light warning to cease and desist the behavior. That could've been your wife walking in on you and not your child. Yet, fifteen minutes later, you text the Side Chick to apologize for the close call and the two of you continue the relationship with tighter security. Now you lock doors when you're in a room by yourself and you've never done that before.

It reminds me of the story of King David that we mentioned back in Chapter 2. There was a red light that he also ignored and it cost him and others dearly.

As a refresher, the story is told in the Bible in Second Samuel 11 and 12 that one day David decided not to lead his troops in battle, but instead to stay at home in his palace at a time when King's especially were supposed to be at war.

David sent his troops off, and stayed home and took a nap. Following the nap, he took a stroll up on the roof of his palace and from there he saw one of his female neighbors bathing outdoors in her outer courtyard. As David looked intently at the suds roll down her nude body, instead of turning away and going back into his palace where he had multiple wives of his own, he continued to stare.

In fact, he stared until his stare turned into an insatiable desire for the woman he watched bathe herself. So, David inquired about who the woman was from a member of his staff. (Here comes the red light), "Sir, that is Bathsheba, the daughter of Eliam and the wife of Uriah the Hittite."[1]

Warning, warning, warning! Stop sign, stop sign, stop sign! Red light, red light, red light! David, that's somebody's wife. And not just *anybody's* wife and daughter. Let me tell you who this woman was. Eliam and Uriah were two of David's top 30 warriors or mighty men. And Eliam's father was a man named Ahithophel who was one of David's most trusted advisors. So, this was one of his advisor's granddaughters, one of his best soldier's daughters, and another one of his best soldier's wife. So you know David's gonna chill. Right? That's three clear stop signs! Leave it alone Bro! Go back to sleep. She's not single and you're already married. So just go back downstairs and go in the house. In fact, why don't you get on your horse, and go to work where you're supposed to be anyway?

Well if you remember what happened next, David ran that red light. He told his staff to bring the woman to him, he forced himself on her, impregnated her and created a royal mess.

A mess he soon tried to cover up in numerous failed attempts to bring her husband home from war to sleep with her so that it would appear that the baby that she would deliver would be Uriah's and not his. But Uriah wouldn't cooperate with David's scheme, and David ultimately had Uriah killed so that he wouldn't have to deal with the consequences of his own selfish choice.

There's not a person alive who's ever had an affair that didn't run through some red lights to go through with it. If you're reading this right now and you're at the brink of crossing the line or you're in a relationship that has moved towards crossing that line, I want you to know that all of those "close calls" of almost getting exposed, are opportunities for you to make the most of God's grace and mercy so you can escape the pending severity of consequences that ignoring those red lights will one day cost you.

Let's check back in on Sandy and Ray.

CHEAT DAY

In the world of nutrition and fitness, there is something called a "cheat day". The idea behind the concept is because you eat clean for 6 days a week or 29 days a month, you have earned one day when you can eat things that are unhealthy to *reward* yourself for all of your hard work, faithfulness, and discipline.

Something similar happens in the world of Side Chickology and infidelity. After all of the days, weeks, months or years of faithfully enduring a bad or sad marriage, it's cheat day. After all of the secret conversations with your new love or lust interest, it's cheat day. After all of the close calls and red lights that you have sped right through, even if a Red-Light Photo came in the mail in the form of a cell phone bill, proving that you have been up to something inappropriate, it's cheat day. After all of the calculations and risk management thinking, and after all of the checks and balances and talk of the big moment, cheat day has arrived.

I'm not a romance novelist or an erotic love storyteller, so you'll have to imagine the details of cheat day yourself. But the sex is always amazing on cheat day even if it's clumsy or less than spectacular, because what the two of you have that is stronger than the sex is emotional intimacy and chemistry. The sex just solidifies the bond.

For some at this stage, the thoughts and plans to leave your marriage and spouse that once were just occasional are now in full bloom. The two of you have gone all the way. And now that sex is a part of the relationship, it tends to be a regular component of the relationship moving forward.

For others, particularly men, all they wanted was the sex and fun, and there's no real interest in leaving their marriage and family for it. It's just seconds for a man with a big appetite.

Regardless, the husband now goes into even deeper levels of hiding. He has more and more unexplained times of absences where he is un-accounted for. He has unanswered cell phone calls from his family, and his excuse is always the same, "My phone was dead" or, "I can't get cell phone service in that part of the building where I work."

Although he may continue to say all of the right things at home with his mouth, his body language and facial expressions are telling a different story.

A second cell phone is purchased with the bill going to another address or P.O. Box to hide the relationship. Both the man and the Side Chick are smitten by the pleasure of the relationship. In fact, what makes affairs so hard to get out of and stay out of is how euphoric the secret relationship is.

You're both usually at your best when you're together. You look your best, smell your best, act your best, and do your best. You don't calculate and pay bills together. You don't deal with disobedient children together. You don't have to manage car maintenance problems together. You usually don't have to smell each other's morning breath, dirty laundry, flatulence, or post-work-out body odor. It's all wonderful when the two of you are together. It's like a movie or video game or an amusement park or spa. It's an escape from reality into a world of dangerous fantasy.

The Side Chick's nails are usually manicured, her feet are pedicured, her hair is done, and her clothes are just right.

The Side Slick's cologne is fresh, his facial hair is groomed, and his car is clean with new car fresheners strategically placed throughout to create an aromatic paradise.

But then there's the other side of his life, the world called reality. His family life... In his family life, he has children with learning challenges. He has financial pressures and arguments over money and how it's being spent. He has in-law drama and complaints over time spent with single friends. He has unresolved arguments and unhealed hurts in the marriage that neither spouse has the tools to fix. He has frustration over a sex life that went from hot and heavy during dating to lukewarm and light and eventually cool and casual in marriage. He has isolation, distance, and silent violence as days go by without significant, safe, affirming, and loving conversations. What a contrast between those two worlds. Miserable at home and happy as can be with Side Chick Sandy.

And many men try to juggle these two worlds as best they can. And in order to keep the fun of the extra-marital affair, while maintaining their allegiance to their marriage and family, they find themselves in the words of song-writer, William Bell "Trying to Love Two".

When a man is infatuated with the lure of an affair, the time, stress, pressure, and demands of that relationship rarely cross his mind. But anyone that's crossed that sacred line of fidelity will tell you that bill was much higher than the budget.

One of those hidden costs is the fear of who knows. At the end of the day, although a man may know that he hasn't revealed his inappropriate relationship to anyone, he really can't be 100% sure whether or not his Side-Chick has confided in one of her girlfriends about the relationship. If she has, who exactly is the person that knows and therefore has some potentially very damaging information about him?

This raises the dichotomous nature of an affair when you consider the fact that two people have to *trust* each other to not disclose their *distrusting* activity together.

Then there's the fear that just maybe in all of their sneaking around, no matter how scrupulous they were about it, somebody may have saw him and the Side Chick together in a way that would raise questions. But who? Who knows? Who? This could torment a man.

Which brings up an additional "bill", the cost of innocent people being thrust into this messy situation. For example, in the story of King David that we've referred to a few times in this book, we learn in 2 Samuel 11 & 12 how members of David's staff were forced into his sordid circumstance to aid and abet him and then to cover up for his reckless choices.

His staff members were the ones who inquired about Bathsheba and went to seize her on behalf of the King, and it was Joab who set up the execution of Bathsheba's husband Uriah at David's written request.

Nowadays we have people who didn't make the choice of infidelity, but are paying a price for it by association and connection with those who are violating their marital vows. It's those innocent bystanders who are babysitting children during secret getaways. These are the people sending warning notifications regarding clued-in spouses, and watching people climb out of windows and using other escape routes to avoid detection. It's a dangerous, reckless game for all involved.

Then there's the time bill. Infidelity is terribly time-consuming. It takes a lot of time to groom and direct and serve and volley an innocent and harmless relationship into an affair. It takes time to coordinate multiple schedules to set up times of sexual infidelity. It's not just coordinating the schedules of the Side-Slick and Side-Chick, they must also work around the schedules of their spouses and all of the children and other demands in their lives to connect in very tight and narrow windows of availability.

Then it takes time to actually have sex with each other. Then it takes time to cover up everything that it took time to plan and time to carry out so that there is no indication to anyone that any of that took place. It's like having an additional full-time job, and hiding by nature is very stressful.

Then there's the impact on one's professional work and deliverables when distracted or consumed by an extra-marital relationship. How productive and professional can a person really be, when they're more excited about a potential direct message and text from a Side-Slick or Side-Chick than they are about the work that they do? Optimal performance, in that case is improbable at best and more than likely impossible.

Then there's the emotional price of living a double life. The Emotional Cost of living a duplicitous life is very hard to quantify because it impacts us on a level where there are no measurements. It's a matter of living conflicted, having an ongoing internal disturbance. When a person is always on the lookout and always on edge, it's very soul disturbing and emotionally disruptive.

Then there's the cost of mental anguish as it finally begins to sink in why we're so frenetic about hiding and covering up everything. We're working night and day to keep the behavior un-exposed because of all that's at stake. The career is on the line. The marriage is hanging on the edge of a precipice. The business is at stake. The family is on the chopping block. Our legacy and reputation are at risk. In some cases, a person's public service and ministry could be permanently jeopardized. That's sobering.

THE POWER OF ADDICTION

The sad reality is many people want to stop this downward spiral of pleasurable but dangerous behavior, but stopping seems impossible. Once an addictive behavior has you in its powerful clutches, breaking free is terribly difficult. If you're wondering whether or not you have become addicted to something, here are some signs and symptoms that usually reveal addiction:

- Time consumption. As stated before, a lot of time is invested and essentially lost in addictive behavior and the time is spent in three separate but connected phases. First there is the time it takes to plan our inappropriate behavior. Preparation, location, etc. are meticulously thought through and planned out because you can't just flippantly do something that is unacceptable. Arrangements must be made in the pre-behavior phase. Then, there is the time that it takes to actually do the inappropriate behavior that we've spent time planning

to do. Finally, there is the post-behavior time it takes to sanitize the evidence and cover the fact that the behavior ever happened. We arrange alibis, erase text messages and phone calls. We make sure that we're home when the mail arrives every day in order to intercept cell phone bills before they are discovered and inspected by our spouse. We take showers to eliminate the fragrance of the other person, etc. Addiction takes time.

~*Expenses.* There are always financial costs associated with addictive behavior. The cost of gas burned in a vehicle to get to the Side Chick or Side Slick. The cost of special grooming, haircuts, hairdos to impress the other lover. The cost of special attire that's worn publicly and privately for occasions together. The cost of sex toys, special fragrances, hotel rooms, airline tickets, dinners, travel expenses, a private apartment, and other expenses to finance the secret rendezvous.

~*Failed attempts to stop.* Another sign of addiction is when you said to the other person, "I am cutting this relationship off. It's not right, so we have to stop," but after a few days or weeks, the affair is back on hotter and heavier than before. Soon there's another verbal commitment to end the inappropriate relationship, that lasts temporarily, and again, it's back like it never ended.

~*Duplicity.* Another symptom of addiction is an internal feeling of duplicity when you feel hypocritical and incongruent. For many, it's a demoralizing feeling when your values and your behavior are not aligned. You feel phony and fake, and it tends to affect your self-image.

~*Unfocused and unproductive.* People who have an addiction tend to add less value to the organizations that they serve and that employ them than they do when they are sober and living with integrity. So much attention in their life is given to either planning, doing, or hiding and covering up what they're doing, that they don't have enough mental energy to do their jobs at an optimum level.

~*Anxiety.* It is very stressful emotionally to manage a relationship that could cost you so much, especially when you're doing everything you can to avoid the "bill" becoming due. You just never know if or when you're going to get caught, and what the fallout will be. This disturbs not only a person's sleep at night, but their ability to rest at any time.

If you can relate to any or all of the above symptoms, it's highly likely that you're addicted, and you're going to need more than just willpower and desire to get out, you're going to need a circle of accountability, support, and a change of environmental factors to help get you out and keep you out.

*In my message entitled "Breaking Bad Habits, It's All in My Head" I deal with both the neurology and spiritual aspects of recovering from addictive behavior. Download it at www.sagacitycompany.com

The irony of all of the factors that I've just described is that in spite of how costly and expensive it is to have a Side Chick, some men have multiple Side Chicks at the same time. Some of them are in the same area, while some are in different parts of the country and world, depending on their resource base and their careers. Some men even have multiple children and families, and they have worked extremely hard to keep this secret world undisclosed. You talk about stress. But the rush of secrecy, is in itself, so addictive that it's nearly impossible to stop without the whole thing experiencing the devastating crash of exposure. Indeed, some men can't get out until they're caught. Ironically, the thing they feared the most, exposure, ends up being the way out of that maze of duplicity and shame.

Another major cost of infidelity is the impact on family relationships that takes place when a man is distracted by an extra-marital relationship. This happens when the man is home, but also not home at the same time. He's in the house, but his interests are elsewhere. Like the lyrics to the old O'Jays song, "Your body's here with me, but your mind is on the other side of town."

When a man is distracted by another woman, his interests are divided. He can't give his full attention to help with his child's homework, because he's in his Side Chick's DM box.

He is not fully attentive at his child's sporting event, even though he's physically present, in fact, he may have even driven his child to the game, but every now and then, he drifts off and away from the field of play, talking on his phone because he got a call from his Side Chick.

There are various household repairs and jobs that need to be completed that continue to go unaddressed because so much of his "free" time is consumed by his feelings, thoughts about, and conversations with the Side Chick.

Because women are naturally very discerning, the wife usually knows that something is not right, even though she's not exactly sure what it is, especially if there's been no previous history of infidelity. But then something goes wrong…

Many affairs are revealed because of some security/protection glitch. The Side Chick and Side Slick, after being so meticulous about covering themselves, had a lapse in "defense", and one of them forgot to erase their email history or left their DM open by accident on social media, and the discovery brought their spouse to tears and rage.

Here we go…

Affirmations

I will be accountable to my spouse and any requests for access to my phone or electronic devices will be granted without push back.
(He who has nothing to hide, hides nothing.)

I will respect red lights and stop any proceedings or conversations that are leading me to betray my marital covenant.

*There are many of you reading this book that have an awful lot at stake that can be squandered by an illicit act or relationship. In my message entitled, "Don't Blow It" you'll hear ways to avoid compromising everything you've achieved or can achieve by falling prey to promiscuity or infidelity. Download it at www.sagacitycompany. com

CHAPTER 6:

UH-OH, THE CAT IS OUT OF THE BAG

Proverbs 5:3-14

3 *For the lips of an immoral woman are as sweet as honey, and her mouth is smoother than oil.*

4 *But in the end, she is as bitter as poison, as dangerous as a double edged sword.*

5 *Her feet go down to death; her steps lead straight to the grave.*

6 *For she cares nothing about the path to life. She staggers down a crooked trail and doesn't realize it.*

7 *So now, my sons, listen to me. Never stray from what I am about to say:*

8 *Stay away from her! Don't go near the door of her house!*

9 *If you do, you will lose your honor and will lose to merciless people all you have achieved.*

10 *Strangers will consume your wealth, and someone else will enjoy the fruit of your labor.*

11 *In the end you will groan in anguish when disease consumes your body.*

12 *You will say, "How I hated discipline! If only I had not ignored all the warnings!*

13 *Oh, why didn't I listen to my teachers? Why didn't I pay attention to my instructors?*

14 *I have come to the brink of utter ruin, and now I must face public disgrace."*[1]

Those words were written over 2,400 years ago and they are just as applicable today. Think about how many men especially, are facing public disgrace because of infidelity and sexual misconduct.

The impact of the exposure of an affair is hard to describe. All of the injuries and damage and sometimes even fatalities at the scene are painful to even write about.

The irony of how this part of Side Chickology unfolds is the fact that as I mentioned in the Introduction, there's a 95 percent denial rate whenever a person is confronted with evidence of their infidelity. Don't expect the truth right away.

Most people will even get animated in their denial of unfaithfulness when they are questioned about the nature of their relationship with someone, exclaiming, "Are you serious!? Absolutely not! I don't even find him/her attractive! Why are you always thinking the worst about me!? Maybe **you're** the one doing something shady! All I do is go to work and come home. I don't have a life. I go to work, do my job, get in my car, drive home, and come in the house, and listen to you complain every night. That's it. Anything else you're conjuring up in your little head is a lie!"

The reason why people are that adamantly dishonest about their behavior is because they have been in "cover up" mode since the affair began. So, if you confront them and catch them off guard, and they haven't even had a chance to inform the Side Chick or Side Slick of your discovery, for the sake of the "team" that they've formed with the other person, and for the protection of all involved, they go deeper into cover up mode and denial.

The only problem is, the evidence is usually too much to successfully deny.

But there's another way the cat gets out of the bag so to speak, and it's not when a spouse discovers infidelity, but it's when the Side Chick needs to meet with you face to face. You're not sure what it is, but it doesn't sound like a "quickie". When you meet up, she's shaking and crying as she gives you the news, "I'm pregnant". The plot thickens…

If she's married, your initial thought is, "Is it my child? How can she know who the father is if she's been sexually active with me and her husband?" And who will the child look like if she goes through with the pregnancy?

If she's single, and she chooses to keep the child, "I will now have another child in this world to provide for." What a tangled web we weave.

I am fortunate to pastor a church that has multiple locations. At the time of this writing Zion Church has an Internet campus, a Landover, MD campus, a Woodbridge, VA campus, a Fort Washington, MD campus, and we're in the process of opening a Campus in Greenbelt, MD. I am able to lead a church with multiple locations because I have a Lead Campus Pastor in charge of each campus. Those key leaders, have staff and volunteers that help them to lead and serve each campus. It doesn't really divide me or cause me to be conflicted, because they run, lead, and serve each Campus.

Well it doesn't work that way, when you have ongoing intimate relationships with multiple women who have each mothered your children. You can't staff that my friend. Essentially, you now have four domestic jobs. You're a husband to one woman. A boyfriend or Side Slick to another woman. A father to you and your wife's children. And a father to your Side Chick's love-child. Wow! You talk about being spread thin. How are you going to manage not only several women at various locations, but also multiple children at different residences?

Whenever a man is divided, he has great difficulty reaching his life's destiny. You have to be focused and decisive to reach your destiny. But infidelity distracts and divides and everybody is getting a part of you while nobody and nothing has all of you. Not even your purpose has all of you.

In spite of the fact that this kind of outcome is always possible, none of these potential consequences were enough to stop the affair from happening or continuing because we just rolled the dice hoping that we wouldn't crap out.

Then there's yet another way the cat is let out of the bag. When the Side Chick gets mad with the Side Slick. She either gets angry with him for lying to her about something, or for not keeping his promise to leave his wife for her. She then gets frustrated with her ambiguous place in his life, and starts disclosing the relationship to others and getting looser with the privacy of it.

In fact, if she discovers she's one of several Side Chicks in his life, and that he's got a 3-piece Side Chick meal with white and dark meat that's spicy and mild, she'll really be tempted to expose the whole thing. Because once the Side Chick has had enough of her Side Slick's lying and deceit her agenda completely changes. It's ironic because the entire relationship was built on lies and deceit, but when she realizes that he's just as unfaithful to her as he is to his wife, she begins to *feel* used. The problem is, she was being used the whole time.

Now that she's "woke", she will ensure that this no good, unfaithful, conniving man is exposed for the selfish person that he is. At this point, the side chick will contact the wife and reveal the affair. Some will put this information in writing, but others will avoid any written documentation to protect themselves in the future and will instead choose to talk by telephone.

THE PHONE CALL

The cat out of the bag phone call, goes something like this:

Side Chick: "Hi, is this Marie?"

Wife: "Who am I speaking with?"

Side Chick: "You don't know me, but we need to talk. I'm sorry to call you like this, but I felt that you needed to know that your husband has had an intimate relationship with me off and on for over six years now."

Wife: "What!? Who is this? And how did you get my number?"

Side Chick: "I'd rather not say my name, and I got your number from Ray's phone. His pass code is 7327. He has an iPhone with a picture of a Philadelphia Eagle's helmet on the home screen. You all have been married for 16 years and your daughter Ariel is 14, your son R.J. is 12, and your daughter Miya is 8."

Wife: "Is this some sort of joke or prank?"

Side Chick: "I wish it was, Marie. I wish it was… Listen, I'm not a tramp. I know better than to conduct myself in the way that I have with your husband, but he was so deceitful to me making me think that you all were not together and that he was going to marry me and this, that, and the third. But it turns out he was using me and you, because I found out that I'm not the only person that he's dealing with outside of his marriage."

Wife: "Where do you know him from? Do y'all work together? The gym?"

Side Chick: "I really don't want to say where he knows me from because I'm only calling you to let you know the kind of man you're married to. Quite frankly I don't know if the two of you will team up on me and use this against me. I don't have anyone to protect me. So, if you don't mind, outside of giving you my name and where I live and work, I'll tell you everything else. He'll probably tell you everything else about me at some point."

Wife: "Okay, well how did you meet him and how long have you known him? (Turning to her youngest child), she says, "I'm sorry sweetie, Mommy's on the phone right now, ask your sister to help you, and I'll come up and check on you to make sure it's right. Okay?"

Side Chick: "I'm so sorry to disturb you and your family with this, but I thought you should know. If you'd like I can call you back at a better time."

Wife: "No, now's a good time."

Side Chick: "Well when Ray and I first met, he told me that you two were still married but basically separated from each other while living in the same house. He said that you two didn't sleep together and only had sex like once a year at best. I found out that wasn't true about 8 months later, when he went off on me for calling him at 1:00am one morning saying that the call woke you up. I'm not sure what he told you, but if it's true and you remember that call, that was me. But because he had me in his phone as his friend Steve, you didn't question him about it. We had our first big argument about it because he had led me to believe that you all didn't share the same bed, and he lied at that point and said that you guys had just started sleeping together again."

*Wife: "Well that's **definitely** a lie. Not only have we always slept together but we also have sex several times a month, and that's been consistent throughout our marriage. I have seen Steve's name come up often on his screen over the years."*

Side Chick: "Well that's me. He has a friend named Steve as you know, but they rarely talk. Just another one of his lies. I fell for them too. One of his biggest tricks was when he told me that God sent me into his life. He told me that he knew that God brought us together. You can call me what you want, but I am a very spiritual person, and I take my relationship with God seriously. He would use the Bible and God and spiritual things to convince me that we were supposed to be together, and that he wasn't listening to God when he met you, and that God was trying to stop him from being with you, but God wanted him to father his three children, and on and on he would go with his lies."

Wife: "You know what? This is crazy. I don't believe you."

*Side Chick: "I agree with you, it **is** crazy. But I have no reason to lie to you." Then in an attempt to eliminate Marie's doubts, she says, "I know about your medical problems. I know that you had to have your thyroid removed. I know about the blood transfusion that you had to have following the complicated delivery of your son. At least that's what he told me. I know about the fact that your brother committed suicide and that was never made public to protect his children. I also know about how ever since your brother took his life that your mother has not recovered. She cries every day, and she hasn't even been able to help you with your kids because of her emotional state. I know about how seven years ago, you begged Ray not to leave you when he threatened to walk away from the marriage and how you started trying different things to make him happy like the bubble baths, candle lights, and trying different sexual experiences."*

Wife: "I'm sorry. I have to go, my daughter is calling me. What did you say your name was again?" Hoping this mystery woman would slip up and give her more information.

Side Chick: Ignoring Marie's request for her name, "I understand. I'm sure you'll eventually find out a lot about me. I intentionally didn't block my number so that you can call me back if you need to talk to me further.

This was hard for me, and I'm sure it's hard for you. I'm very sorry."

A DEVASTATED WIFE

Nothing can prepare a woman for that phone call. It leaves her literally feeling shocked and gutted at the same time. Her emotions are at level 1 zillion as she is blown away not just by the infidelity, but by the fact that her deeply private world has been shattered by blatant disloyalty.

I once heard this statement on a Focus on the Family podcast: "An affair doesn't simply break marital trust, it shatters it." It's not a clean break, it's more like a compound fracture rupturing everything in its vicinity. How could something so appealing as a passionate, romantic fling, do such pervasive harm and damage?

How could Ray tell Marie's deepest family secrets to a woman that she doesn't even know? How could he be so heartless? Marie gave her love to Ray. She almost died delivering his long-awaited son. She gave Ray her promise of fidelity and had kept it 100 percent. She trusted Ray with her life and her heart. How could he be so cruel and selfish?

She rushes to her bedroom, locks the door behind her, turns on the television with the volume significantly loud, runs into her walk-in closet, crumbles to the floor, stuffs her mouth with a towel, curls up in a fetal position, and wails from the deepest part of her soul, a cry that's so explosive that it scares her. There she lies, trying to survive this devastating revelation while trying to protect her children from the pain.

I'd like to pause right here and say to every man and woman reading this, *this* is the unseen side of Side Chickology. This is the real consequence of infidelity. – Indescribable pain.

In her book, "The State of Affairs", Esther Perel writes (*language warning*),

"The revelation of an affair is eviscerating... the maelstrom of emotions that are unleashed in the wake of an affair is so overwhelming that many contemporary psychologists borrow from the field of trauma to explain the symptoms: obsessive rumination, hypervigilance, numbness and dissociation, inexplicable rages and uncontrollable panic. Treating infidelity has become a specialty among mental health professionals… in part because the experience is so cataclysmic that couples can't manage the emotional fallout alone and need intervention if they hope to make it through.

In the immediate aftermath, feelings do not lay themselves out neatly along a flowchart of appropriateness. Instead, many of my patients describe swinging back and forth in a rapid succession of contradictory emotions. 'I love you! I hate you! Take your shit and get out! Don't leave me! You scumbag! Do you still love me? Fuck you! Fuck me!' Such a blitz of reactions is to be expected and is likely to go on for some time."[2]

Marie has now been thrust onto an emotional roller coaster that she'll have to ride for quite some time while trying to balance everything else in her life. And the ebb and flow of her emotional waves will go from devastating hurt to seething rage. She'll go from thinking, "How could he do this?" to "I want to kill him!"

"Victims of an affair often feel an overwhelming sense of suspicion toward their spouse. Everything is interpreted through the lens of betrayal – their spouse's choice of clothing, their phone conversations, even the slightest deviation from their daily routine. In fact, the feelings of doubt can be so compelling, that many spouses will check in on their partner repeatedly throughout the day in an attempt to monitor their every move.

To someone who has been emotionally devastated, such behavior seems rational. It's an attempt to take charge of circumstances that seem wildly out of his or her control. The trouble is, it doesn't strengthen a person. It actually weakens him. Tracking your spouse's every movement will keep you trapped in a cycle of fear and suspicion, which will only drive you into deeper depression and higher levels of stress. This doesn't mean, however, that you should give your spouse carte blanche for the future or dismiss the need for healthy accountability. In fact, the guilty party must be willing and agreeable to reasonable measures of accountability. Real healing and reconciliation can't occur unless he or she is ready to be open and aboveboard about all of their comings and goings and social interactions. Trust may be restored if accountability is maintained over a long period of time, but not otherwise. That's just the way it is.

If you're in this situation, the thought of releasing control of your spouse may seem terrifying. But in reality, there is only one person you can control: you. That's not to mention that, ultimately, there is only one Person you can trust: God. Somehow or other, you have to get to the point where you can leave your spouse and your marriage in His hands."[3]

ANGER IS A SECONDARY EMOTION

Anger is rarely the very first thing we feel in any given situation. Anger usually follows shock, fear, hurt, disappointment, or rejection. The anger is often equivalent to the initial pain. It's a defensive emotion that aggressively protects us from whatever or whoever injured us.

The problem with anger is, the fact that it's such an explosive emotion that it can do as much or more harm than the harm that caused it. It is very retaliatory in nature. Oftentimes we believe that the only way to stop the pain is to eliminate the person or situation that caused it. We think, "If I don't have to see his face, smell his scent, or hear his voice or name ever again, I can move on with my life."

Infidelity produces and maintains tormenting emotional pain that's very hard to shake. It makes a person question and doubt themselves. "Am I not good enough? Sexy enough? Pretty enough? Handsome enough? What do you need that I'm not giving you?" The self-blame and guilt alone can drive a person crazy.

Then there's the constant crying when the memory of the infidelity comes up, even months and years later. Something triggers the memory and the tears and fears start to swarm the soul of the betrayed spouse.

Indeed, sin will take you further than you want to go, keep you longer than you want to stay, and cost you more than you want to pay.

Affirmations

I will leave other people's husbands and wives alone.

I will protect my family by being faithful to my marriage.

CHAPTER 7:

THE PRICE IS WAY TOO HIGH

Infidelity is almost impossible to hide in a home because the natural outcome of the damage impacts everyone.

Daughter: (To a constantly crying mother.) "Mommy, why are you crying?"

Mom: (Trying to protect her daughter from the truth.)

"Oh baby, it's ok. I was just thinking about your Uncle, my Brother who passed away."

Daughter: "I'm sorry Mommy. It's ok…" (Rubbing her back.) "Mommy, where's Daddy?"

Mom: "Your dad's busy at work Sweetie. Have you tried to call him?"

Daughter: "Yes. He says the same thing you said. He says, he has to work a lot and that he'll be home soon." Then there's that question that rips through your soul that comes from the lips of a child who doesn't know all of the details or repercussions, "Are y'all getting a divorce?"

What do you tell a kid, who sees their mommy constantly crying, and only sees their dad here and there, and they ask you, "Is our family going to be officially and permanently demolished by divorce?"

Once again, Marie has to protect her children while her own soul is hemorrhaging in pain.

Mom: "I hope not, Baby. I hope not. It's going to be ok. Mommy and Daddy will always be here for you." And her instincts move her to protect a man who didn't protect his marriage and family. "Your Daddy loves you. He and I just had a few problems that we needed to work on. But he loves you and your brother and your sister. It's going to be alright. Just pray, okay?"

Daughter: "Yes ma'am."

May I ask everyone that's experiencing this book a simple, rhetorical question right here? What sex is worth this kind of pain imposed upon innocent lives?

When the reality of an affair is exposed, oftentimes more and more of the ugly truth comes out over time as the betrayed spouse continues to research and ask questions about the details of the inappropriate relationship. Many times, this research reveals that there were "meetings" and "conversations" and "texting" going on with the Side Chick during very personal and sacred times in the marriage. These discoveries can further intensify the emotional pain of the betrayed spouse.

Furthermore, the pain of infidelity makes an individual very sensitive to emotional triggers for years to come when something reminds them of that painful period in the past.

Then there are the counseling costs. It is pretty much impossible for a couple to navigate successfully through the trauma of infidelity without professional guidance, wisdom, and accountability. The time and costs of this necessary support often needs to be in the budget and schedule for several months or even years before things are stable again.

However, even with counseling, sometimes the bridge from betrayal to trust seems too far for the betrayed spouse to cross and it often takes too long in the mind of the unfaithful spouse for the betrayed spouse to get there. This is why constant arguments regarding the affair keeps coming up.

But many people don't understand that forgiveness is not a moment, it's a journey. If this is hitting home for you as a man or a woman, whether the marriage relationship is salvaged or not, in order to live the rest of your life whole and not bitter and broken, forgiveness is a must, not solely for the betrayer, but even more so for the one who was betrayed.

"Forgiveness is about letting go of our anger toward someone who has hurt us. This can be tough for some people because they've confused "forgiving" with "excusing". They have the idea that they're being forced to consider the wrong done to them as acceptable. But this is not true. Forgiveness never waters down the awful nature of an offense. In fact, forgiveness really isn't about the offending person at all. Instead, its purpose is to release the heart of the offended party from the resentment that often accompanies emotional pain."[1]

*If you are struggling to extend forgiveness to someone or with being patient as you seek forgiveness from someone, you can download my message here called "The Journey to Forgiveness". I go in depth on the subject of forgiveness and how it's distinguished from trusting a person again. Visit www.sagacitycompany.com for the download.

Another cost of infidelity is the ongoing difficulty that the unfaithful spouse has remaining faithful moving forward because in spite of all of the pain his choices have caused, remaining on the road of purity and fidelity seem nearly impossible for him. That's because he's now either in love with someone else, addicted to the inappropriate behavior, perpetually plagued by euphorically recalling the affair, or all three. So sometimes, emotionally, he doesn't know if he's coming or going. He's constantly bombarded with the conflicting feelings of desperately wanting to return to a relationship and environment that nearly cost him everything valuable in his life. Who can he tell this dark truth to? Not just the fact that he was unfaithful to his wife, but the fact that he sorely misses his Side Chick.

Sin is like credit card debt. The transaction may be pleasurable, but the payments often continue for years.

That reminds me of the financial costs of divorce which can devastate a family. One study revealed that after divorce, women experience a 27 percent decline in the quality of their standard of living.[2]

Legal fees are astronomical. Custody battles take an enormous toll on everyone. The dividing of assets is tedious and painful as well. To watch and experience the dismantling of a family construct over infidelity is arduous.

No wonder God says that He "hates divorce." Here's exactly what He says in Malachi 2:11-16:

> *[11]Judah has been unfaithful, and a detestable thing has been done in Israel and in Jerusalem. The men of Judah have defiled the Lord's beloved sanctuary by marrying women who worship idols. [12]May the Lord cut off from the nation of Israel every last man who has done this and yet brings an offering to the Lord of Heaven's Armies.*
>
> *[13]Here is another thing you do. You cover the Lord's altar with tears, weeping and groaning because he pays no attention to your offerings and doesn't accept them with pleasure. [14]You cry out, "Why doesn't the Lord accept my worship?" I'll tell you why! Because the Lord witnessed the vows you and your wife made when you were young. But you have been unfaithful to her, though she remained your faithful partner, the wife of your marriage vows.*
>
> *[15]Didn't the Lord make you one with your wife? In body and spirit you are his. And what does he want? Godly children from your union. So guard your heart; remain loyal to the wife of your youth. [16]"For I hate divorce!" says the Lord, the God of Israel. "To divorce your wife is to overwhelm her with cruelty," says the Lord of Heaven's Armies. "So guard your heart; do not be unfaithful to your wife."[3]*

Then there's the ultimate potential cost of infidelity; someone's life is ended. The darkest side of Side Chickology is the reality that sometimes it ends in tragic violence and death. Heed the wisdom of the Old Testament sage in Proverbs 6:27-35:

> *[27] Can a man scoop a flame into his lap*
> *and not have his clothes catch on fire?*
> *[28] Can he walk on hot coals*
> *and not blister his feet?*
> *[29] So it is with the man who sleeps with another man's wife.*
> *He who embraces her will not go unpunished.*
> *[30] Excuses might be found for a thief*
> *who steals because he is starving.*
> *[31] But if he is caught, he must pay back seven times what he stole,*

even if he has to sell everything in his house.
[32] But the man who commits adultery is an utter fool,
for he destroys himself.
[33] He will be wounded and disgraced.
His shame will never be erased.
[34] For the woman's jealous husband will be furious,
and he will show no mercy when he takes revenge.
[35] He will accept no compensation,
nor be satisfied with a payoff of any size.[4]

Infidelity is always dangerous, but the stakes rise to another level of recklessness when the relationship involves a married woman. If you're a man and you've gotten "involved" with a married woman, or you're getting close to one, please consider what's at stake. If nothing else, just consider how you would react to a discovery that your wife was having a sexual relationship with another man. Sir, is it worth the risk?

History is replete with cases of married men who can't forgive their wives infidelity and in an attempt to get revenge, commit a double homicide, killing their wife and the wife's lover, and they eventually commit suicide because they can't see themselves living beyond this pain either. All you have to do is Google double homicide/murder – suicide love triangle and one story after another heart-wrenching story appears.

Sometimes the betrayed spouse goes through so much personal shame over the discovered infidelity that they suffer with ongoing feelings of inadequacy. They often make comparisons between themselves and the other person physically, professionally, socially, financially, etc., sizing them up, and often feeling more and more depressed.

Again, sometimes there are thoughts of self-blame like, "Maybe I deserved this." Sometimes the betrayed spouse is so devastated and hopeless emotionally that they want to harm themselves and take their own lives.

Infidelity doesn't always end in violence, but there's still always a cost.

There's the "For Sale" sign in the yard, and it's there because the home that once housed a family, is now the object of negotiations in a courtroom. All of the memories, past hopes, dreams, and prayers prayed in that house are now buried in its foundation.

Family events will never be the same. Mom and Dad will never be "together" again at any event, even if they're both in attendance. Now children will have to get used to going to separate areas at the event to interact with each parent.

Sporting events will never be the same. Now parents will sit in separate sections of the stands, sometimes with their "new" love interests, sometimes alone. Then there are the awkward interactions with coaches and parents and the whispers that are spread amongst the other parents like, "They're not together anymore? I notice they don't wear wedding rings anymore. Is that the Side Chick he's with? That's so sad…"

If you're a married man engaged in an affair, or you're headed in that direction, I'd like to ask you a question. Have you considered the fact that if you keep going in that direction that one day your children may call someone else "Dad"? Or that someone else will be living in your house with your wife, sleeping in your bed with your wife, taking your children to school, disciplining your children, and giving them fatherly advice?

Has it dawned on you that there's a possibility that some other man will be tinkering around in your garage, responsible for keeping your lawn manicured, and getting his mail out of your mailbox?

Have you considered the real possibility that some other guy will be watching football in your favorite chair in your man cave on your television with your remote control and even having some of his buddies over while your wife brings him chips and beverages on a tray?

I can assure you that no one is thinking about these costs when the tennis court flirting is taking place.

What about in your "new" family that you chose over your original family because you and the Side Chick decided to end your marriages to marry each other? Did you expect to have all of the blended family complexities that now exist? Did you expect to be repeatedly disrespected and even feel threatened as a man by the ex-husband? Did you expect your former Side Chick, now wife, to have so many personal conversations with her ex-husband in the name of matters regarding the kids? Did you expect your new wife to ever admit to you that she honestly misses her family although she loves you? Did you expect to hear the step-children yell back at you, "You're not my father!" when you tried to discipline or correct them? Or for them to exclaim, "I wish you would get out of our house so that our father could come back! Why don't you go back home to your own family? Why did you break up our family?!"

You see, no one brought these costs up while all of the sexting and secret rendezvous were going on.

What about all of the transition and adjustment costs and the toll those costs have on everyone involved. Like finding a new Church when the infidelity causes there to be a relocation, or there are circumstances that involve members of the same church. What about having to find new schools for the kids, when divorce requires a geographical move, which also places the kids in a new community and neighborhood away from their friends, classmates, and teammates on local sporting teams? Who calculated these costs?

What about the social cost of being constantly judged for leaving your wife even if you end up marrying the side chick. The cookout whispers, "So that's who Ray left Marie for?" And now there's this perpetual shade cast on the new relationship which leaves you with the constant feeling of shame and judgment whenever you're around people who knew about your previous life and how the life you're now living all came about. The costs continue to add up.

Going back to the legal costs, what about the shame that happens in a courtroom when all of your dirty laundry is aired out in a public forum like that where everyone else that happens to be in the courtroom can see it? What about the guilt and shame of tearing down her character, her emotional and mental stability, and other disparaging things that are said and done in divorce proceedings to protect your own image and to justify abandoning your family and breaking your marriage vows, promises, and covenant? So now on top of devastating your wife with infidelity, you now choose to destroy her with vindictive and harmful words in a public setting. How could you be so heartless?

How about the cessation of family traditions like nighttime prayers and bedtime rituals that gave your kids a sense of safety and protection? The end of family trips and vacations in the minivan filled with laughs, adventure, and junk food. What about the family games like hide-and-go-seek, tickle monster, and playing in the sprinklers? Never again.

Because children need strong family roots to grow and develop, this disturbance of their foundation can have an enormous social and emotional impact on them. Amy Morin says that "Young children… may worry that if their parents can stop loving one another that someday, their parents may stop loving them."[5]

Then there's the cost of a complicated family tree with multiple, complicated branches. "Is that your sister? That's my half-sister? My brother and I have the same mother but different fathers, but my sister and I have different mothers but the same father. I stay with my Father and my half-sister, and I also have two step brothers, (my step mother's children) that live with us during the summers. And I stay with my mother, my older half-brother, and my little half-brother that my mother had with my step-dad. Folks, who calculated this when we were sliding in each other's DMs?

I had the child of a Side Chick tell me once that she felt semi-orphaned. She literally said to me, "Where do I belong? I'm the result of sin." It was so sad to hear this adult woman ask that question about herself when she had nothing to do with the way she arrived in this world. Yet she was plagued by the shame of her origin and the secrets that still surrounded her life as an adult.

Affirmations

Doing what's right is more important than doing what makes me happy.

Infidelity is not in my family budget. No thanks.

CHAPTER 8:

SOMETHING TO THINK ABOUT

If you've been operating in the role of a Side Chick or Side Slick, or you're contemplating being in that space, here are some things worth considering. The Good News Translation of Galatians 6:7 says,

⁷ Do not deceive yourselves; no one makes a fool of God. You will reap exactly what you plant.[1]

What goes around, comes around. Since that's true, and since it's also true that you probably want a marriage of your own one day that is loving and faithful and free from infidelity, make sure you are protecting the future of your own potential marriage by protecting other people's marriages and leaving their spouses alone.

In other words, respect yourself and your future enough to stop participating in or moving towards any adulterous relationship. You must love yourself and your future enough to end an inappropriate relationship, knowing you're going to reap what you sow.

Respect the institution of marriage enough to not engage in a relationship with a married man or woman. Your ultimate desire should be relationship exclusivity and your behavior and choices should be aligned with that desire. Don't settle for second, because if you don't stop being second, you'll never be first and only in someone's life. Second is a mentality.

In professional baseball, there are generally two types of pitchers on each team, starting pitchers and relief pitchers. The starting pitcher sits in the dugout during the game with the rest of the team, while all of the relief pitchers sit in another part of the field in a section called the bullpen. The relief pitchers are only called on to enter the game when the starter is tired or is not getting the job done. Oftentimes it's late in the game when the relief pitcher is called upon, and many games, he's not asked to come into the game at all.

When he is called into the game, it usually starts with a phone call from the dugout sending a message to warm up. And sometimes the relief pitcher warms up and is never asked to enter the game. Because they are back-ups, they don't know from day to day whether they'll get in the game or not. And on those occasions when they are actually called into the game, the manager of the team doesn't call them by name, he makes a gesture either on his way to the pitcher's mound or while he's standing on the pitcher's mound, pointing to his left arm or right arm, which distinguishes which relief pitcher he wants for this particular moment.

That MLB scenario is analogous to the life of a Side Chick. She doesn't live with or sit with the team that she's called in to serve from time to time. She's not a starter (wife), she's relief. She often gets calls late in the game (evening) and those calls are often indications that her man(ager) is not satisfied with his starter, and he's looking for some relief. When he reaches out to her, he uses codes to describe what it is he wants in that moment, and she happily obliges because she's just happy to get in the game.

Now I'm certain that there will be those that will pick that analogy apart and argue against its efficacy, but my point is simply to challenge you to place a higher value on yourself as a woman. Don't tolerate being someone's relief pitcher; instead require an exclusive, monogamous relationship.

Likewise, I'd like to challenge men who are either practicing Side Chickology, (the act of engaging in an extra-marital relationship with another woman) or they're contemplating engaging in Side Chickology. Could it be that you can literally ruin two brides by that self-centered behavior?

You can ruin the bride you married by your betrayal and infidelity and you can ruin the "bride" that never gets married because she was always waiting on you. Meanwhile, you selfishly tied her up with the false hope of a future that you knew deep down inside you would never provide her with. Two brides ruined by one man. Or is it three? Or four you've ruined?

Here's another thought to consider as we use some forward thinking to anticipate some of the many inevitable outcomes of infidelity. What happens when you run into old friends? What happens when that friend asks you and the Side Chick that you left your wife for, "How'd y'all meet? How'd y'all get together?"

You might give them the fake version. "Well we were co-workers and really didn't know each other outside of an occasional hi and bye. But after we both went through a divorce, we just became good friends. Neither of us were really looking for a relationship since we were both still working through our divorce issues, but we discovered over time that we had a lot in common, and decided to go out, and the rest is history."

Then there's the real version. "Our daughters played on the same basketball team, and he used to walk us to our car after practice and games if our spouses weren't there. Oftentimes, because of our family schedules, only one of us could make the practice or games, while the other one supported our other children. We were both married at the time, but he always treated me special, and I didn't have that in my marriage. So, we started using our daughters as an excuse to have extended conversations with each other, but because we were part of this AAU Community we started being discreet about it, and began texting and calling each other during game trips, and even during games to keep our growing interest and attraction to each other discreet.

"On one of the trips, we decided that his daughter would stay in the room with my daughter, and one night while the girls were sleep, at around 1:30am, I texted him to see if he was still up, and I snuck out of my room into his, and that was the beginning of a sexual relationship that evolved out of our emotional closeness. We worked hard for months to try to hide our relationship, as both of our spouses had their suspicions about us. In fact, my ex-husband confronted him once regarding our relationship and asked him if anything was going on and he lied and denied it and said everything was on the up and up. That brought us a little more time, but to be honest, I wanted him to confess everything and just rescue me from my empty marriage but that didn't happen.

"It wasn't until my ex-husband eventually hired a private investigator who caught us on video kissing passionately, that the truth really came out. Upon that discovery, my ex-husband went off. I thought he was going to literally kill us. I have never seen rage like that in my entire life. He called my current husband's ex-wife and told her everything, which set his house upside down emotionally. My ex-husband also told my current husband's employer, and sent them the videos from the investigator. My current husband worked as an Administrator for a Christian School during that time. He was immediately terminated.

"My ex-husband sent out a graphic email to all of the parents of the AAU program as well as to all of my family members, and to members of our church, with photos of us in compromising situations. It was pretty bad and very embarrassing. I wanted to disappear. I certainly didn't want to be seen in public. I felt like a tramp. But at the same time, I loved this man (referring to her former Side Slick and now husband) and no one knew 'our' side of the story and how miserable we were in our marriages. So, we both separated from our spouses, and moved in with each other while going through our divorce proceedings. We both went through very ugly divorces and custody and asset battles."

SOMETHING ELSE TO CONSIDER

What happens when you run into old friends from years ago and they ask about how your wife is doing, referring to your ex-wife because they think you two are still married? *Fake version* – "Oh you know Debbie and I got a divorce man. Yeah, it's been about 8 years now but it's all good. We're both in a much better place now. Best decision I ever made. I'm happily remarried. I mean don't get me wrong, Debbie's a great woman, you know her. I have nothing bad to say about her, but we just grew apart man… We tried counseling, the whole nine yards, but at the end of the day, you know you both have to want it man, and we just decided to go our separate ways but be there for the kids, and man it's worked beautifully. We have joint custody. The kids LOVE my new wife. All is well Bro. How are you and your family doing?"

Now the problem with this popular but fake version is the fact that divorce is never that pleasant and smooth. The answer leaves out a lot of the painful details because it's intentionally defensive in nature. That reply is an attempt to protect the person giving the response from exposure and accountability for the parts of the story that were deliberately left out.

Here's a real version of an answer to that same question: "Man Debbie and I are no longer together. Yeah. I got involved with a lady I knew from years ago, and I came across her Facebook page and started liking and commenting on some of her pictures. And that evolved into us messaging each other on Facebook and exchanging phone numbers. We decided to have our first public reunion/encounter at a bar where the meeting could seem coincidental to any observer that might know us. Mind you, this was all happening while things in my marriage were pretty bad, and I started having an inappropriate relationship with her without my wife's knowledge. By then, I was living in the basement and pleasuring myself with pornography almost every day, and when I hooked up with this woman, I felt like a new man. So, I eventually told Debbie I was unhappy and that I was leaving and going to get my own place and try to do something that might bring us both some happiness. I told her there wasn't anybody else in the picture, but I think she always knew. She begged me to stay, even promised to make whatever changes were needed to save our marriage and family. She asked several times to go and meet with her pastor for counseling and everything, but by then, man, I was gone. My body was at home, but my heart, mind, and soul were in another place. To make a long story short, the whole things has crushed Debbie, and the kids have had a rough time adjusting, especially Cameron. He's been getting in trouble at school, fighting and what have you. But I couldn't keep living a lie man, so I went through with the divorce. My family has written me off. My mother told me God is not going to bless me until I repent. My father has just stopped speaking to me. He doesn't want to watch sports with me or anything. Just nothing there. My sister and her husband came over to my apartment and did a prayer ceremony and put holy oil on me and they even told me about their struggles and how they worked through them. The Divorce Court judge didn't like me from day one, and took me to the cleaners and gave everything to Debbie so if it wasn't for my new wife, I'd be homeless. By the way, I remarried. I pretty much lost my job because of it because not only did everyone at work love Debbie, but I missed a lot of days at work because I was so into this new relationship that I would take off for days to go on trips and even do stay-cations with her. Plus, it was hard to face my co-workers every day, knowing what was going on in my personal life. So, it's been a rough journey man. I've lost over 30 pounds because of the stress. I've struggled with depression and I'm alienated from my family. I really miss my kids, man. I really miss them and I missed out on so much of their lives. It would've been cheaper to keep her on so many levels, but I was in love."

Then there's another issue that Side Chicks and Side Slicks often see but overlook and that's the issue regarding the other person's children. Let me ask you Sir/Ma'am, do you really want to be bothered with someone else's kids? Really?

If Side Chicks and Side Slicks would be honest, they would admit that more often than not they want the person but *not* those kids! Unfortunately, it doesn't work that way. The Side Chick/Slick and the kids are a package deal, including all of the drama that comes with those rascals.

What happens when you try to correct or admonish one of those package kids and they yell at you, "Who do you think you are!?"

What happens when your lover tells you, "I love you, but I don't put anyone before my children. They have been hurt enough by what happened to their father and me. I refuse to make them think that I'm going to leave them too. My kids come first!"

Now here you are, right back where you were in Chapter 1. You're in second place again! That's why you started dealing with this Side Chick who's now your new wife, that you left your wife for, because you were second, and now you're back in second place again. Wow!

Oh, and what about those infamous ex-spouse private phone

calls? What happens when every time the step-kids' dad is on the phone with your former-Side Chick-now wife, that she often walks away from the room to talk to him because he's irate about something again? I mean how secure do you feel living in a home with an angry man's children and his ex-wife? How much sleep can you get at night knowing that he's 'out there somewhere' wishing you the worst, especially if for some reason you end up living in his old house? That's incredibly unnerving.

The ex-spouse has given you the nickname "Buster" because he says you busted up his family. So naturally you feel pretty helpless when he calls your wife angry about something, and even though the anger is stressing her out, what do you look like protecting his ex-wife, which is now your wife, that you took from him? (Seems a bit *twisted* don't you think?)

How time consuming and emotionally and mentally exhausting is it to have to wait until your wife gets off of the phone with her ex to have her try to explain to you everything he's upset about? This leaves you frustrated and conflicted at the same time. On one hand, you're angry that the ex-husband won't just move on with his life. On the other, you're also feeling guilty that your choices created this conundrum.

How about this realistic scenario: What happens when you and your new wife have a special trip planned and just hours before it's time to head to the departure point for your romantic cruise together, the ex intentionally disappears and is not responding to calls in spite of their promise to keep the kids? So, there you are with thousands of dollars invested in a non-refundable trip and suddenly no childcare. Strangely enough, after losing the money and the opportunity to go on the trip because you couldn't scramble up childcare in the final hour, two days later the ex resurfaces and claims they lost their phone and all of their contacts and was stranded out of town. Pay back is mean. But then again, why would we expect an ex-spouse to be supportive of a relationship that ended their marriage, and even serve as a childcare provider for the advancement of that relationship?

To every man reading this book, I have a question for you. Remember Uriah? He's the husband of Bathsheba in 1 Samuel chapters

11 + 12 that I mentioned earlier in the book. He was merely a dedicated foot soldier in the army of a king. A king who took advantage of his loyalty, vulnerability, and ultimately took his wife and his life from him. Fellas, Uriah never did one thing to David. He did not deserve that. It was so cold-blooded that Nathan the Prophet was sent by God to confront David regarding his selfish and reckless behavior and cover-up. What about you today Sir? Could it be that God is sending me to warn all of us men who are either tempted to cross the line of fidelity or have already crossed and need to run back to the other side? What about that husband that never did a thing to you or your family Sir? Give that man his life and his wife back while you still have time.

Here's something else to consider. What are we teaching our children? As parents, we are always teaching our children by the things that we say and by the example that we set. What are we teaching them about commitment and keeping your promise and your word when we walk away from our marriage covenant and vows to do instead what will make us happy? How does that land with a child when we're telling them to hang in there and finish what they start whether it's work, school, music, or sports? If you can't stay committed to a big thing, why should they stay committed to a much smaller thing?

What about the length and breadth of the painful impact caused by infidelity? When an inappropriate relationship is exposed, the damage is immeasurable and difficult to track. Children are disrupted and frightened. The injured spouse is often shocked, devastated, and traumatized. Extended family is disturbed by the news and unsettled by what it means for the future. Co-workers are whispering at the water cooler and simultaneously curious about its development while saddened by its domestic impact. Church members are hurt and experience a huge let down particularly when it's a person of prominence and respect in the church. Neighbors are sobered by it, while internally grateful that it wasn't their family that was hit with the devastation.

Divorce also hurts generational relationships and can cut off connections between grandparents and grandchildren. These are all innocent bystanders that are all painfully impacted by the choices of one or two people...

Then there are those other incalculable expenses to consider, when you take into account all that's at stake. Sometimes entire businesses and non-profits atrophy significantly and even tank when there's infidelity in the C-Suite, particularly when it's the President, Senior Pastor, or CEO. Careers tend to plateau, if not plummet significantly when there's Side Chick activity going on. I've already mentioned the devastation to the construct of families when the line of fidelity is crossed without repentance. Countless numbers of impactful ministries are severely hindered by infidelity. An individual's reputation is smeared by it, no matter how many other admirable things they have done. Oftentimes, it becomes the dominant part of their legacy.

Here's another question worth considering. How do you want to be remembered? The reality is, the longer we live, the more people will reflect on the life that we have lived and the contributions and choices that we have made. So how do you want to be remembered?

I know it can be a bit morbid for some, but I think it's worth imagining your funeral for a moment. If there's a traditional viewing ceremony, while you're lying in that casket with absolutely no control over what's happening around you or in memory of you, consider this question: Who will walk up to the casket and kiss you goodbye? Who will walk by your casket trembling with tears and touch your corpse as a sorrowful farewell? Will it be any Side Chicks or Side Slicks? Will your family have to sit through that? How awkward would that be? Who will need emotional consolation that is a bit over the top and noticeable to all? Will it bring an embarrassment to your family and a blemish on your legacy?

Affirmations

I won't settle for being a substitute or relief for some-one that's unhappy in their marriage relationship.

I will seriously count the cost before I write an infidelity check that could very well bankrupt me.

***(By the way, if you're in a bad marriage, I didn't write this book to suggest that it's ok to remain in a miserable marriage. I believe that we should work hard to turn our miserable marriages into happier ones, and oftentimes we could experience that transformation if we'd do for our spouses what we do for our Side Chicks or Side Slicks. I also believe that surprisingly, an affair and its being exposed could be a major catalyst in improving an empty marriage. I'm going to spend the rest of this book focusing on how to protect our marriages from infidelity, and I'll especially focus on recovering from infidelity if it occurs in Chapter 11.)

CHAPTER 9:

RIBOLOGY

(As you can tell, I enjoy making up "ology" words.☺)

I've spent the better part of this book writing about some of the causes and consequences of infidelity. Now I'd like to turn our attention to some of the ways we can stave off infidelity from our relationships. I certainly don't want these suggestions and recommendations to imply that the war for fidelity in our marriages is not a terribly difficult one. Indeed, this battle is both ferocious and perpetual, so like in any conflict, we have to have a battle plan that will aid us in this epic struggle.

In Genesis 2:21-25 we find the creation of the Earth's first wife. Here's the account:

²¹ So the Lord God caused the man to fall into a deep sleep. While the man slept, the Lord God took out one of the man's ribs and closed up the opening.
²² Then the Lord God made a woman from the rib, and he brought her to the man.
²³ "At last!" the man exclaimed.
"This one is bone from my bone,
and flesh from my flesh!
She will be called 'woman,'
because she was taken from 'man.'"
²⁴ This explains why a man leaves his father and mother and is joined to his wife, and the two are united into one.

[25] *Now the man and his wife were both naked, but they felt no shame.*[1]

Out of all the things that God could've used to create the world's very first woman, wife, and mother, He used a rib. He used dirt to make Adam, but He used one of Adam's ribs to make his wife for him. Why a rib?

Matthew Henry has been credited for saying that ""The woman was made of a rib out of the side of Adam; not made out of his head to rule over him, nor out of his feet to be trampled upon by him, but out of his side to be equal with him, under his arm to be protected, and near his heart to be beloved."[2]

In order to get to Adam's rib, God had to put him to sleep, cut him open, remove the rib, and close up the incision. God performed a C-Section on Adam (well sort-of); pulling the life of his wife out of him.

The process, though maybe not as painful as a surgical procedure equivalent to that today, still would leave Adam in some discomfort and it would also leave him scarred in the place where God removed his rib. In fact, I'm sure that when Adam woke up, he was sore.

In order to gain a wife, Adam had to give up something (a rib). Getting married will always cost you something. And although it's natural to focus solely on what we gain when we get married; (a spouse, a life-partner, a co-parent, a supporter, a lover, a friend, a confidante), it will also cause us to give something up for as long as we are married, that we cannot take back without doing damage to the relationship.

If at any moment in the relationship, Adam ever demanded to have his rib back, that would mean the end of his marriage, because his rib was what he had to give up to have Eve as his wife. Adam's dowry to have Eve was some of his very own flesh and bones.

Think about it. If I took out one of your ribs and some of your flesh and had the capacity to build another human being for you to be connected with in marriage out of that material that I took from you, you wouldn't need me to tell you that it cost you something to have that relationship.

There are some things that we must sacrifice to be married, that must remain sacrificed in order for the marriage to continue. Sometimes it's something that's a deep part of us that has been a part of us for a long time... I mean you've had your rib all your life. In fact, not only did Adam have to give up his rib to be married, but in addition, God told Adam in v. 24 that a man has to leave his father and mother and cleave to his wife and the two of them should be one flesh.

Here's a drum-roll kind of question for you to consider if you're single: What will you have to give up to get married and stay married? Your player card? Your black book? Your being a momma's boy? Your independence? Your separate bank account? Your passcode to all of your electronic devices? Your "friendships" with people who pose a threat to the fidelity of your future marriage? What if keeping something alive from your single life, would be the ultimate death of your married life?

These are significant questions to ask yourself because when you've been single for most, if not all of your life, it's not simple to move from a "me" (single) way of approaching life, to a "we" (married) way of approaching life.

Oftentimes men are perplexed regarding who their soul mate is. "Who should I marry?" is a question that often crosses their minds, primarily because they've got so many options. But if we stay with the rib analogy and consider the fact that your wife will be your "rib", if someone is going to be your rib you can sense what's missing in you, in them. Adam could look at Eve and see and sense that she was what he was lacking.

The totality of Eve's created being fit what Adam was missing. It just fit. That's the best way that I can explain it; it just fits. Things just click between you.

On the flip side, if you're in a dating relationship and it doesn't fit spiritually, emotionally, intellectually, philosophically, etc. Or if your goals are not aligned and your values are not in harmony, don't try to force it to work.

Kellee Patterson used to sing a song that said, "If it don't fit, don't force it, relax and let it go, just because that's how you want it, doesn't mean it will be so."[3]

This is a terribly important point. When you're contemplating a long-term marital commitment to someone, you should ask the question, does this person add a value to my life that would be missing without them? Or am I the only one that's adding value in the relationship, and thus I'm a missionary mate who's coming along to rescue and redeem and restore and uplift this other person?

Relationships that have an imbalance of investment tend to atrophy in intimacy because the one that's doing most or all of the work will eventually get tired. And because those relationships feel more like a parent-child relationship rather than a partnership, the mature partner doesn't always want to be sexually intimate with the immature partner because having sex with a "child" is a crime. Ideally, each partner should be dialed in so that one doesn't feel under-supported and the other doesn't feel under-valued.

In the human anatomy, ribs are covered by skin and tissue. As a rib, Eve came from a place that was always covered. She was created from an internal place, not an external, exposed one. Even naked, the ribs are still covered.

That's why by nature, women long to be covered. They function optimally when there is someone under whose wings they can be covered.

The scriptures teach in 1 Corinthians 11:3 that, "… the Head of every man is Christ, the head of woman is man, and the head of Christ is God." God-Christ-Man-Woman. That's God's creative order and not meant to be sexist, and it doesn't measure either gender's created intrinsic value, it's simply a matter of divinely ordained order. Even the most independent women that I've counseled over the years, long to have a man that will cover and protect them.

A woman needs to know that if something ever happens to her husband that everything is covered. That's probably why it's easier to sell insurance to women than it is to men, because insurance is all about coverage. A woman needs to know is her house covered? Is her car covered? If her children get sick and need to go to the hospital, are they covered? "If I feel uncomfortable about a female friend that you have, will you expose me and tell the friend that I'm insecure, or will you cover me and amend your relationship for the good of our marriage without making me the bad person? If we get caught with forbidden fruit in our hands, will you step up to the plate, confess your mistake before God and cover me, or will you stand back and tell God, it's the woman that you gave me that caused me to do what I did?" By and large, women, desire to be covered.

That's why it's always good for a single woman to have some guys in her life, whether they are family or friends, who look out for her and make sure she's protected and covered. I need to clarify that a woman's desire to be covered by a man does not necessarily mean that she desires to get under the covers with that man as well. It's more of an issue of protection than affection. She wants to know that she's safe and secure.

She wants to know that if she's married and she hears a noise in the house at 3:00am that frightens and awakens her, you will unhook your C-Pap machine, slip on your Crocs, grab a bat and search the house until you assure her that all is well.

Ladies, being a rib comes with relational responsibilities. Anatomically, the primary function of the rib cage is to protect the heart and lungs. You protect your man's vital organs, particularly his heart from things and people that are harmful to him that he may be unaware of. As a rib, you tend to be more aware of intangible danger so we guys need to let you all help us in this way.

Don't bury your head in the sand when you sense danger to the fidelity of your marriage. You're a protector. It's true even in the animal kingdom, for while the "father" of an animal group is out hunting for food, the "mother" of those animals, guards and protects their home and babies.

Ladies, if you've got to scroll through his phone and internet history and ask questions about the nature of some of the relationships that he's in, it must be done because you protect him from blind spots. You see from the inside out.

In the over 30 years that I have been in a relationship with Vicki, she has never been wrong about her distrust of another woman. Never. Even when I blew off her concerns, I only found out later that she was spot on.

Women have insight. They see way below the surface of people and recognize things that endanger the safety and fidelity of their marriage and family.

When a woman says, "I don't feel comfortable with him in our house." Or, "I'm not okay with you texting her at 11:00 at night even if it is work related", that's her radar at work, and it's rarely off whether we want to admit it or not.

If you're married, your wife should have access and passwords to all phones and electronic devices. She's your rib and she protects the vital organ of the fidelity of your marriage. The old saying is true, "He who has nothing to hide, hides nothing."

Ladies, if your husband refuses to cooperate, continues to do whatever he wants to, befriends whomever he chooses, and keeps all of his electronic devices private and off limits to you, then bring it to the attention of people that you all are accountable to that you both respect and honor.

If he still won't change, and you've done all you could to bring this to his attention, you turn him and the marriage over to God, determine your non-negotiables, and stick with them. Any relationship that doesn't have mutual accountability is both physically and emotionally unsafe. A lot of guys, try to justify keeping their wives out of their phones because they claim that she's making stuff up out of everything she sees. That's a bunch of hogwash. (Had to keep it PG). It's just his way of manipulatively flipping the attention back on her, and covering up his slickeration and flirting.

Sadly, a lot of men get away with a lot of unaccountable, reckless behavior for years because they know that their wives aren't going anywhere, especially Christian wives, or wives who aren't financially independent. Many of them don't have careers that could sustain them, so they've put all of their trust in God using this man to take care of them. They've been raising kids, and being a faithful homemaker and don't feel like they have anywhere to go, because they've built their entire lives around taking care of their husbands and children. That's actually an honorable thing, that shouldn't be squandered by the selfishness of us men, by cheating.

Unfortunately, many of these women become enablers because even if they threaten to leave, their husbands know they will always be there for them.

Well, he might need to come home one day, and his wife, the furniture, the mini-van, (or the SUV nowadays), the children, the credit cards, and the checkbook are gone with no forwarding address.

Why? Because if he's not going to let you be a rib and protect him, and instead he keeps placing your marriage and family in danger, you're just getting out of the way so that you don't end up getting hurt with him.

I know that is a terribly simplified summation of a very complex scenario, but I can't emphasize enough that when a man has no consequences for his slickness and unwillingness to be accountable, then the possibility of him stopping that behavior is slim to none.

As committed as I am to the institution of marriage for a lifetime, I believe that there are some women that need to leave their marriages and never return until they get a promise from their husbands to change and submit to accountability to them and others to keep them doing things the right way. Otherwise, the arguments, blow ups, fights, tension, anxiety, and emotional and psychological pain may never cease.

There is another function of the rib and that is the rib cage provides support. Our shoulder muscles, chest, upper abdomen and back are all attached to our rib cage. Without the ribs, our entire torsos would collapse. Ladies, you are your man's biggest supporter.

The truth is what discourages a lot of married men is the fact that they don't feel supported by their wives. So many husbands feel undervalued, underappreciated, un-celebrated, un-loved, and un-wanted at home. This is another version of relational ADD, when a man is experiencing an attention deficit disorder in his marriage, that we discussed in the first chapter.

You see, we as men pay attention to being ignored by our wives, while they simultaneously pour all of their love and attention on their children, their mothers, their girlfriends, their fitness, their hair, their church, their social media pages, or their favorite television shows. Every husband remembers when he was first. He remembers when he was your number one priority. Now, whenever the kids get sick, you sleep in the bed with them. Another child gets sick, and you spend the night at the hospital with them.

But when your husband gets sick, you get on him telling him, he needs to stop trying to do so many things. In his mind he's wondering why you won't climb in bed with him and comfort and nurse him back to health like you do the kids.

Being an NBA chaplain, speaking in NFL chapels, and just being a fan of the world of professional sports has given me an opportunity to see a lot of things. One of those observations has been how certain athletes don't want to play for certain teams and organizations, or they want to be traded. Sometimes it's not because of the front office or their teammates, it's because of the fan base. When a player is competing for a team which has a fan base that cheers more for opponents and boos their own players, even though that player may make millions of dollars annually, he wants out of that environment.

Just like athletes who don't get love from their home fans, any man who's not celebrated at home usually wants to play for another team. If he often hears complaints from his wife, and rarely praises and words of appreciation, he doesn't want to opt in year after year to his marriage. That may sound superficial, but it's real.

In the sport of boxing, two fighters compete inside of a ring for a certain number of rounds. Each round is 3 minutes, and for those 180 seconds, those two combatants are doing whatever they can to overcome and overwhelm each other. Jabs, hooks, body shots, upper cuts, even head butts, low blows, and elbows are used to gain advantages sometimes. And following those often brutal 3 minutes, a bell rings, signifying the end of a round, and for 60 seconds, those fighters get to go to their corners to get rest, attention, advice, encouragement, water, refreshment, etc. The quality of what that fighter gets in his corner is often a huge factor in how well he performs in the fight.

A married man's life is similar to a boxing match. He daily has 3 minutes of fighting in the ring of life -- in society, at work, in school, etc. He's facing temptation, discrimination, unfair treatment, and more in a dog-eat-dog world, and then he has 1 minute of rest, renewal, support, care, love, and encouragement, when he comes home to his corner.

But what is life like for a man who has to fight to succeed at work, fight injustices in the community, fight against systemic issues that are holding him back in society, and then comes home to an environment where instead of getting encouragement, love, comfort, support, and rest, he comes home to silence, indifference, negativity, and complaints? If that's a man's daily experience, he naturally begins to prefer either going to a more supportive "corner" or even to what some might view as a neutral corner, like happy hour at a local bar to prepare to come home to a less than supportive environment.

I'm not suggesting by the boxing analogy that the husband is the only one that needs to feel supported in the marriage. The wife needs support too in order to be at her best. Indeed, there should be mutual support in a healthy marriage, I'm just focusing on the wife's role as a rib in this part of the chapter.

The 3rd function of the ribs is for breathing. There are actually muscles housed between each rib called intercostal muscles. We have internal intercostal and external intercostal muscles.

The internal intercostal muscles in the rib cage helps us with expiration or breathing out, while the external intercostal muscles helps us with inspiration or breathing in. So as a rib ladies you help give us inspiration and you impact our expiration, no pun intended. You can inspire your man and you can help to expire him.

You not only have the power to help us breathe, but you have the power to knock the wind out of us and take our breath away. You can be like oxygen to your man or you can suffocate him. You can literally be the wind beneath his wings or knock the wind from his sails.

*I go into more detail regarding this subject and how we are created differently as men and women in a classic message entitled, "Musings from Eden". You can download that message here at www.

Men, I want us to understand that our wives (ribs) are powerful but they're also delicate. We have to be careful how we treat them so that they function at their highest capacity, which is for our good. Whenever ribs are fractured they don't function well. God made our wives ribs so that we could never break them without hurting ourselves. In fact, guys, have you ever noticed that when we hurt our wives we never really feel good as a result?

Affirmations

As a wife, I will do what I was designed to do and protect and support my man, being his biggest defender and greatest cheerleader.

As a husband, I will cover my wife and make sure that she and my children are provided for throughout my life and even when I die.

CHAPTER 10:

SIDE CHICK PROOFING YOURSELF (SINGLES)

To the Chief Musician. A Psalm of David.
40 I waited patiently for the Lord;
And He inclined to me,
And heard my cry.
² He also brought me up out of a horrible pit,
Out of the miry clay,
And set my feet upon a rock,
And established my steps.
³ He has put a new song in my mouth—
Praise to our God;
Many will see it and fear,
And will trust in the Lord.¹

Whenever an artist or song writer is about to release a new song, they usually don't put out the entire album or CD at the same time. Instead, they'll choose a song on the album that they anticipate will be one of the hot songs, and release it as a single or an extended play song. They'll send out texts and posts through social media encouraging everybody to "Check out my new single". In the world of music, a "single" is a sample of the whole.

When you're an artist who's putting out a new single, there's a sense of pride and enthusiasm that comes with the release of something you worked so hard on that is now ready for the world to experience. After all of the mixing and all of the laying of tracks in the studio; after all of the layers of labor from concept to reality; after recording, re-recording, and re-writing verses, and changing nuances to make sure the song would be its very best, the moment arrives when you can finally say, "Please go to Sound cloud, i-Tunes, or my website and check out my new single."

It's really a great accomplishment when you think about it, and it's an exuberant feeling to know that all of the time and money and energy has paid off and is now revealed in a 4- minute song.

In the Old Testament Book of Psalms, author, musician, and song writer King David writes in Psalm 40:3, "God has given me a new song." In fact, if you ever read through the Book of Psalms, you'll see David say that a number of times.

Indeed, David is responsible for many of the praise and worship songs that are sung in churches all over the world even to this day. Artists have been sampling David's lyrics for years! If David's descendants got credit for all of the songs that have come from his Psalms, those royalty checks would be abundant.

In this particular Psalm, it's amazing how the results of what God brought David *through* in verses 1+2 ended with a song. One of the gifts or pearls that came out of his pain was a new song. I can only imagine that one of the most exhilarating things that a song-writer can experience is to be inspired with a new song.

I was talking to a popular song-writer in my area once about him coming back to our Church to perform again, and he lit up when he said, "Let's wait until the summer time. I've got something coming out in June that's going to be off the chain!" He then went on to say, "I'll probably release a single off of it in April or May."

When he told me this, I didn't sense that he was being arrogant or self-serving at all. I simply saw him as an artist who was just thrilled about the new songs that he had been blessed to receive and now he could share them with the world. Personally, I think that's awesome.

Similarly, when David says in Psalm 40:3 that God had given him a new song, I can feel his excitement. Although I'm sure he wrote songs during good times, and he probably wrote songs during regular times, what seems special about this one, is that it came following a really difficult time in his life.

After he was crying out to God in verse 1 and after being in a slimy pit of mud and mire as he described it in verse 2, he says, God stabilized him and set his foot on a rock, and gave him a firm place to stand. Then David says, He gave me a new <u>song</u>. Not an album, not an entire CD. But *a* song. A single.

It's got to be pretty cool, when God brings you through something dark and deep and difficult and out of that matrix of misery, you arise victoriously and with new lyrics and music. I think that's true in many ways for all of us, even those of us who aren't poets, or lyricists, or song writers. When we go through something challenging and tough, to come out of it whole and with a song is awesome.

The thing that has always intrigued me about this particular song that David got from God, is the way that he said that people would experience it. Most songs are written and recorded to be *heard*. Music is an auditory genre. Songs are for our ears. Nobody says it smells like music to my nose or it looks like music to my eyes. People usually say, "It sounds like music to my ears."

But David said, that this song, which he received after the storm, would be *seen* by many. How ironic, given the fact that there was no MTV or BET or VH1 at this time. Indeed, video was not a part of the music genre until the 20th century. Yet, almost 3,000 years before music videos, David said, this new single would be "seen".

CHECK OUT MY NEW "SINGLE"

I started thinking, what if we could borrow that terminology from this Psalm of David as well as from the world of music entertainment and apply it to single people? What if every unmarried, never married, widowed, or divorced person, could have a new or even a renewed mantra for their singlehood?

Maybe you've been single for a while, but moving forward, what if the way that you approached your singlehood changed in positive ways? What if in your *new* single, you lived with even greater focus and intentionality? What if you were more purposeful in your singlehood?

So much so that although there are many people who have heard and seen some of your old *"records"* as a single, this new "project" and version of you would be much different and improved. Having come out of your own studio of suffering, you have a whole new song, and people won't just hear it because talk is cheap, but just like David's song, they're going to see it in your life.

So, if you'd allow me to co-write this song with you, the following are nine verses that I recommend be a part of your new single.

VERSE 1 - I KNOW THAT I AM WORTHY OF THE VERY BEST LOVE.

In Romans 5:8 we read "But God showed his great love for us by sending Christ to die for us while we were still sinners."[2]

The historical death of Jesus Christ was the most paramount act of love in human history. The solemn decision of Holy God to make Jesus the substitutionary, atoning sacrifice for the sins of all of humankind is so astonishing, that for some it's literally unbelievable. But it happened and God intended it, and without it, we would be eternally doomed and lost. And the amazing thing about it is that, we did absolutely nothing to earn it. It was totally a demonstration of the love of Almighty God.

Since God thought you were worth that kind of love, then you are truly worthy of the very best love in your earthly relationships. You don't have to settle.

I love the amazing vocal ability of the late singer Luther Vandross, but there's one of his love songs that I'd have to respectfully disagree with. In his song, "Any Love", he says,

Everyone needs a love no doubt
Any love, any love...[3]

I beg to differ. If God thought we were worth dying for and

literally loved us to death, then we're worthy of more than *any*, inconsistent, secondary, uncertain love. Friend you're worthy of more than somebody loving you when they get around to it or when they have time for it. You are worthy of somebody's focus, time, energy, and attention to details. You are worthy of someone's money, investment, thoughtfulness, and consideration. You don't have to accept a part-time lover, a lover for hire, or a contractor lover. You are worthy of a full-time, fully vested, fully committed kind of love.

No matter what life or people have said to make you feel otherwise, you, my friend are worthy of being in a loving relationship with someone that's grateful to have a relationship with you. Not somebody who is just putting up with you.

I remember speaking at a relationship event once where I was asked to address an audience of singles as well as young married couples. During an interactive part of my session, when I was fielding questions, one gentleman said while sitting next to his significant other, "I didn't get what *I* wanted in a person, I got what *God* wanted for me." And although I'm not at all assuming that he meant ill intent by his comment, to publicly say before hundreds of people with the person he's referring to sitting right next to him, that she's not what he wanted for himself, but what God wanted for him, reduces her down to some humbling, tolerable assignment from God, instead of being the best thing God could've ever done for him.

If you're in a dating relationship with someone who views you that way, love yourself enough to escape that emotional prison of under-appreciation, because ***I know that I am worthy of the very best love.***

VERSE 2 - I WILL LOVE MYSELF ENOUGH TO TAKE CARE OF MY SPIRITUAL AND PHYSICAL HEALTH AND FITNESS.

This means that I will take time to prioritize me and my relationship with God. I will begin my days connecting with God and taking care of my body. I will eat more whole foods like fruits and nuts and vegetables and cut out junk and processed food. I will make time for exercise. I will put myself on my calendar and make time in my schedule to love myself. Before everyone else gets a *piece* of me, I will bring my whole self to God and do spiritual and physical exercises that bring me to my optimal health spiritually and physically. Then I can serve those who depend on me from a place of stability and wholeness. A lot of people are depending on me and are making regular withdrawals on my time, energy, ideas, knowledge, wisdom, creativity, gifts, talents, resources, and abilities, and I can't continue to bless others when I'm not investing in myself. I will not neglect me. Not for another person, a job, a church, a group, or anything.

Years ago, I heard a well-meaning Christian leader say that the way to find real joy in life is to follow the acronym J.O.Y. Put Jesus first, others second, and yourself last and you'll have joy. Well that looks nice and sounds cute but it's not healthy. Even on a commercial aircraft we're told that if there's a problem with cabin pressure and there's a need for oxygen, to make sure that we put on our own oxygen mask before we try to help even our own children with theirs. That's because a person who is suffocating can't help someone else until they're in a good place.

My greatest contribution to others in my life whom depend on me is to take care of myself so well that I bring my best self to them for service. Otherwise if I'm trying to fill others up and my own emotional bank account is empty, then life will continue to write checks against me that I am unable to cover, and the overdraft fees will be felt by all.

VERSE 3 – I'M NOT TRYING TO WASTE MY TIME.

Once you know that you are worthy of the very best kind of love, you stop wasting time with people who are playing games. By the way, people typically play with things that they don't intend to own. We rarely treat things that we rent with the same care and value as we treat the things we own or desire to own. Therefore, the fact that you would find yourself in a relationship with somebody who's literally playing games with you is an indication that you're in a relationship that's ultimately wasting your time.

And when I say, "playing games" I'm basically referring to the person who wants the benefits of being in a relationship with you but doesn't want to make a public and legal commitment to you. They have a surfeit of reasons and excuses for why they can't move forward toward commitment, and are allowed to continue to put your life on hold.

Friend, time is such a precious commodity that once it's used, it can never be re-captured. Every second that ticks away in our brief lives is time that we can never retrieve. Time is uniquely precious, for if I do something that wastes my money, it's frustrating, but I can get more money. But if you waste my time, it's gone forever. I can't get that back. The truth is, none of us really knows how much time we have left, no matter how healthy and fit we are. And since a relationship is very time consuming, when you know that you are worthy of the very best love, you guard your time against foolishness. Allow me to elaborate on this verse in your new single.

What are some indicators to let you know your time is being wasted and you're dealing with foolishness? Fellas, you're dealing with foolishness when a woman gives you her number, yet every time you call her, she's never available to talk, and she never returns your call. Moreover, if every time you call, she asks, "Who is this? (This is Steve) Can I call you back?" and she never does, she's not interested and she's wasting your time. Just the fact that your name and number are not stored in her phone is an indication that you're someone that she doesn't have a problem acting perfunctory toward.

Have you ever called a company or some kind of service-oriented place and you get an automated voice? The way that automated voice communicates to you tells you a lot about how valuable you are to the company that you're calling. If you hear something like, "Due to the high volume of calls, please try again later", and then you hear a click, followed by a dial tone. And when you call back an hour later, you hear the same automated message, click and dial tone. Newsflash: when this happens repeatedly, you're not valuable.

However, if you hear, "Hello and thank you so much for calling. Your call is very important to us, so please stay on the line. We're experiencing an unusual amount of calls but your call is important to us and will be answered in the order in which it was received. Your estimated wait time is 4 minutes, please remain on the line and someone will be with you shortly." Then they play some music for 30 seconds and come back again, saying, "Thank you for your patience, please continue to hold and someone will be with you momentarily. Again, please excuse the inconvenience, and thank you for holding." Now that's someone who values you and your time. And if you're anything like me, waiting is still uncomfortable, but it's a lot different when you know that you and your time matter to the person you're waiting for.

What I'm saying is, how many cold shoulders do you need before you get the message, that the person playing games with you is not interested in you? Move on with your life. Delete their contact information and love yourself enough to not allow their games and mistreatment to diminish your self-worth.

Now there are those occasional relationship stories of the person that kept pursuing someone after being turned down repeatedly, and the two people end up getting married, but that's the exception not the rule. When you're in a relationship that's worthy of your time, and it's the right fit, you don't have to force it.

Sadly, some of you reading this book have been on hold in relationships for years! He told you years ago he was going to leave his wife for you, and every month he's got a new reason why he hasn't done it. Yet, because you have clung to the euphoric hope of one day living happily ever after with him, you can't muster up the courage to walk away from months or even years of waiting. Move on with your life and in the words of Congresswoman Maxine Waters, "reclaim your time."

To the guys, let me give you another secret to knowing if someone is worth your time. Assuming you've gotten to a place where you want more than just another person you can have sex with. Assuming you want to go beyond, just having sexual conquests to another level of a meaningful, substantive, deep, heart-level, loving, committed relationship. One of the ways you'll know you're with someone who is worth your time and who understands that you are worthy of the best love, is after you have met and exchanged contact information, by the second time you go out with her, if not the first, she will know almost everything about you. Unlike the "game player" who re-asks you your name every time you call, this woman will have already done major research on you through every source and resource available to her. It's not to stalk you; it's to do a thorough assessment on you. Before she goes all in and puts her heart into the relationship she's got to know what you told her, and what you didn't tell her.

By the time of your second conversation, she would've Googled you, run a criminal background check on you, checked out all of your social media pages, read your posts, scrolled through your followers, surveyed your bio, checked your LinkedIn account, asked her girlfriends' police officer boyfriend to look into who you are, contacted an old high school friend that went to college with you about you, and researched your zodiac sign to see if you two had chemistry. Brother, she darn near has a downloadable app on you by your second conversation. She is not playing around.

Ladies, how can you know when you're dealing with foolishness and someone that's wasting your time? Interestingly enough, it doesn't take very long at all to know you're dealing with a time waster. You can know you're dealing with foolishness just by the way a man approaches you. If he hollers at you with or from a group of guys he's with, he's wasting your time. For example, if you walk by a group of guys, and one of them says, "Hey beautiful. Hey, can I talk to you for a minute?" Just save your life from the immature drama and respectfully keep walking. That behavior from a man reveals several things. Number one, he's probably the alpha male in his group. Number two, he may be the one with the most relationship confidence. Or number three, it means he's simply trying to impress his friends by flirting with you. Number four, it probably also reveals that he likes what he sees, which is not always a bad thing. But number five, what it absolutely reveals is that he will most certainly waste your time.

Here's why: Whenever a man finds you physically attractive but he's not interested in a relationship with you, he will say something to you that lets you know that he's only focused on what he sees and what he may be able to get from you. He's simply objectifying you.

On the other hand, when a man is physically attracted to you and he is so taken by you that he immediately places you on the kind of pedestal that would make him feel honored to have a relationship with you, he really won't know how to approach you. That kind of respect is not confident, it's actually awkward and a bit clumsy. I don't care how smooth he is, his "game" will be completely turned off at that moment because he's not playing games at that point. So, at best, he can get off an awkward "Hi" to you or something like that. And he's hoping like crazy that he will run into you again and that's okay. because most quality relationships require more than one interaction.

What I'm trying to say ladies is that if he can approach you with various lines like, "It must have really hurt when you fell from heaven" and "I've got a terrible headache because you've been walking around in my head all day." If he hits you with that kind of flow and smooth talk and it's all witty and flirtatious, he's revealing to you that he's going to waste your time if you let him. You can't be so desperate for attention that you will be willing to play that game.

Any man who really views you as worthy of his best love will really not know how to approach you initially. He'll just wave or sheepishly make eye contact. His nervousness and awkwardness are signs that he is serious. Even if he's not nervous and awkward, he will not approach you with some canned, rehearsed one line pick up statement. He will approach you with awe-filled respect.

VERSE 4 - IF IT'S DOWN LOW, IT AIN'T FOR SHO. (BY "SHO" I MEAN CERTAIN.)

Sometimes you have to draw a line in the sand and declare, "I'm not tolerating any more secret relationships. I'm not going to keep hiding my relationships from the people who genuinely love me and care about me. If it's a relationship that's worthy of my time, then it's a relationship that doesn't need to be hidden. When it's right it can be revealed. I'm not keeping my relationship life hush-hush anymore. I'm not letting my 'boyfriend' continue to introduce me as his platonic friend in public when he wants to have sex with me in private. I'm not going to keep meeting him at hotels where we don't check in together. I'm done with parking my car around the corner and going up back staircases to avoid detection. Any relationship that can't go public, can't be right." Secret relationships are often selfish relationships. Usually, one or both parties want the relationship to remain a secret so that they can have the benefits of the relationship without the public accountability of the relationship.

Fellas, when a woman is serious about you and the relationship, she *wants* to meet your mother. She has nothing to hide. In fact, that's the best way that she can gather more information about you, understand you better, and love and support you more effectively. What better way to secure that important intelligence regarding you than an interview with your mama?

Your mother has the pertinent files. Meanwhile, any woman who is not interested in meeting your mom or your family, is not serious about you or the relationship, or they have something to hide, including their relationship with you.

Ladies, the same is true for men. If he never brings you into his genealogical world, then he's hiding you and the relationship, which means this relationship is uncertain and is quite frankly a waste of time.

This verse in the new single song is not intended to be in opposition to the discretion needed in the early "just getting to know you" stage of a relationship. I do believe that there is a period during the embryonic stage of a courtship where it is premature to publicize the nature of the relationship, because it's still very much uncertain how and where things will go, if anywhere at all. Even then however, there's always someone in your life who is close enough to you that should know what's going on with you. That kind of accountability is important in my opinion because infatuation has a way of making us a bit stupid, and we always need someone reasonable and wise in our lives to keep us grounded.

Furthermore, the old saying that "love is blind" is true. When you fall in love with someone, it's very easy to not see things that other people who are not in love with the person see very clearly. If you keep your relationship out in the open for people that love you to observe and see, they can give you their honest assessment of the person and point out some things that you have missed or ignored.

Relationally a part of your "new single" is the fact that you're looking for someone that will show you off, not hide you. You want someone who, everywhere you go, will say, "Hey Fred, have you met my Girlfriend?" Or, "Hey Missy, have I introduced you to my Boyfriend?"

Whether you're attending a sporting event, or while you're shopping in a store. In restaurants, at movie theaters, or at the gym working out together. Whenever you see someone you know they say, "Hey let me introduce you to my boyfriend or my girlfriend." You're done with being in the closet about your relationships.

Now why is that so important? Because one of the keys to a healthy relationship is exclusivity. You need to tell everybody you know that "This is my significant other", just in case, they are "unfaithful" to you and they're "out" with someone else and you're not around. At that point, your 'eyes in the community' can help you hold them accountable because the relationship is public.

The next verse comes from a minister that I heard speak from Baton Rouge, Louisiana named, Louis Greenup:

VERSE 5 - NO WED, NO BED. NO CONTRACT, NO CONTACT.

I have a new single and I don't want to be on just anybody's hit list, just so they can boast about how much they are getting from me.

This may sound a bit antiquated in a world where sex seems to be as popular as food, but I truly believe that in a non-marital context, promiscuity creates ambiguity.

Whenever we're being led by our groin, instead of our brain, we end up doing things that are not prudent.

The brutal truth in many cases is the fact that there are some people that you have sexual relationships with that you know beyond a shadow of a doubt that if the sex was not a part of the relationship, you would not be with that person. So, what greater way to get to a level of clarity and reality than through chastity and celibacy? Just as promiscuity creates and feeds ambiguity, celibacy brings clarity.

Ladies, you want to know if he feels like you're worthy of the best love? Then don't have any kind of sex with him and see if he stays around. If after several attempts to seduce you and convince you to "make love" to him, you still don't give in, if he starts saying stuff like, "I just need some space. I just have to get my head together. I need some time to just work on me." Welp, now you know.

It may hurt to discover the truth that you were convenient, but not priceless to him. And although you may have to cry yourself to sleep for many nights, at least you aren't having sex with someone that doesn't feel like you're worthy of the best love.

Let me tell you something that I'm totally convinced of. Some of you reading this book would be surprised at how many people out there that would love an opportunity to offer you the very best kind of love. People who would value you that much, but they've been unable to because they know that you're in a relationship. You need to release your new Single this year and let everyone know. Like Nicki Minaj once said, "It's true everyone, I'm single and I'm coming out with some new music." So, check out my new single.

VERSE 6 I WILL NOT BE A "MISTA-CAL OR MS-TERY".

(That is Mystical and Mystery in case you missed it.)

I think there are people who for whatever reason, enjoy being strange. I personally believe that weird behavior is their way of masking their lack of self-esteem. They act like someone unique in order to stand out, since they tend to evaporate into the culture when they act normal. But in this new single, it's important that you conclude that "I'm done with these unclear, mystical, uncertain, mysterious relationships and people. If you want to try to act like you're different and interesting, playing a role in a Movie that never stops, you go right ahead by yourself. I'm going to be me and I'm going to be clear.

Sir/Ma'am aren't you tired of all of the faking and fronting and perpetrating? At what point do we take off our masks and costumes and all of the other things we use to cover our flaws and say, "Here it is. The good, the bad, and the ugly."

Progress demands transparency. If we can't be honest with each other about our true selves, true struggles, true origins, and true brokenness, then we aren't going anywhere. And if we aren't going anywhere we don't need to be together, because I can be stagnant alone. Why do I need your help being stuck in my life?

VERSE 7 – I'M NOT GETTING HIGH ON SHALLOW RELATIONSHIPS ANYMORE BECAUSE I NEED TO BE SOBER ENOUGH FOR A DEEP AND MEANINGFUL ONE.

Some of us are with people because we know at any time we can get a hit from them. They thrill us and get us high, even without the use of alcohol and drugs. Whether it's because of their money or their bodies or their popularity or whatever.

We continue to connect with them because they medicate our emotional pain, loneliness, emptiness, disappointment, and feelings of inadequacy, but we really don't want to marry them. In fact, if the truth be told, they're just a fellow relationship crack-head just like us. We're both just fantasy addicts, waiting on the opportunity to use each other for our next high. Desperate for another hit. It's hard to view someone as a mate when they're really just a fix.

When a person is always "high" on whatever they get high on, even if it's getting high on another person, they tend to miss out on quality, substantive relationship opportunities because they were busy either chasing down a high, setting up a high, getting high, or crashing from a high.

You've got to be sober in order to connect with somebody who is well, because healthy people don't attract sick people into their lives. In fact, if you keep attracting sick, emotionally unavailable, self-centered people into your life, it's because either you're a professional therapist who gets paid to help them, or it's because your "old single" is still playing on the stereo of your life and all of your viewers and listeners know that you're far too desperate to not let them in your life.

That's why you had to come out with a new single and it has you so focused on being whole and healthy that you don't even want to be around sick people.

If you've ever had the flu and you know what that's like, and God brings you through it and out of it, and you're healthy again, if you walk into a room with someone and they're coughing and in pain and they tell you, "I've got the flu", you'll be out of that room faster than a New York minute.

The same is true in relationships. If you've been in one sick addictive relationship after another or even just one for that matter, and God brings you out, even if He dragged you out and you were kicking, screaming, and crying because you really wanted to stay, once you get healthy, you do not want to be around that stuff again, because you can't be available to a healthy relationship when you're constantly in a sick one.

VERSE 8 – I WILL NOT BE YOUR MOTHER OR YOUR FATHER. I'M LOOKING FOR A GROWN MAN OR GROWN WOMAN, NOT A CHILD.

Some of you made church noises and statements when you read that verse like "Umph", "Whew", "C-mon", "Well", "Amen". You know why? Because you're sick and tired of being in relationships with immature, insecure, sensitive people who can't be challenged or told the truth. They don't want to grow intellectually, they don't want to grow professionally, they don't want to grow financially, they just want to play spades, video games, and Jenga.

Your mantra should be, "I will not be loaning you money because you don't have the discipline to save money for difficult times. I will not co-sign on a car loan for you. I will not co-sign on a small business loan for you. I will not let you put an apartment in my name because your credit is bad. It's time for you to grow up. If you want to blow your entire paycheck on your hair, shoes, outfits to go to the club every weekend, and not make sure you have enough for childcare, that's on you.

If you want to buy weed and beer and football game tickets, food to tailgate, and team jerseys without making sure you have money set aside for your rent, your insurance, and your car note, I'm not doing that this year. Grow up.

I've got enough kids, and nieces and nephews of my own, I don't need to be dating a kid. I need a responsible, mature, grown man or woman. I'm not interested in being your parent, I'm looking for a partner.

VERSE 9 – IF YOU'RE NOT FULLY SINGLE, I'M NOT DATING YOU.

"If you're not unmarried, widowed, or never married, you are not available, and I'm not crossing that line. If you're married, you're off limits. If you're separated, you're still off limits. If you're going through a divorce you're still off limits."

It happens every single day. Someone falls intimately in love with someone that's not completely out of their marriage, and it ends up biting them in the rear end down the road. They're either hated by the person's family and accused of tearing apart the family, or they're dragged along for years waiting on the person to finally get out of the marriage, and it never happens.

This may be one of the hardest verses to live out in your new single, but if you could muster up the conviction, boundaries, and courage to only engage relationally with fully single people, it will protect you and others from a lot of pain. Declare this, "I want my own potential husband or my own potential wife, and right now, you aren't available to be that. Furthermore, I don't want us to just stay in touch or just be friends in the meantime while I wait on you to end everything. That move is old, and it's not wise. If I'm around, still single, and available when you're fully single and available, fine. But I'm not putting my life on hold or sharing you emotionally while I wait on you to be free legally."

Affirmations

I deserve a love that is public and pure and I won't settle for anything less.

I will practice celibacy so that I can have the clarity that I need to make sound decisions relationally.

CHAPTER 11:

SIDE CHICK PROOFING
YOUR MARRIAGE

In my opinion marriage is one of the most important decisions we'll ever make. The word 'decision' is no small thing. Dr. Dan B. Allender, in his book, "Leading with a Limp" says, "To decide requires a death, a dying to a thousand options, the putting aside a legion of possibilities in order to choose just one. De-cide. Homo-cide. Sui-cide. Patri-cide. The root word *decider* means 'to cut off.' All decisions cut us off, separate us from nearly infinite options as we select just one single path."[1]

When we decide to get married it means that we are bringing an end to our single life and our availability to others, and beginning our exclusivity to one. Making that decision means that some things and some people need be cut off and cut out of our life.

Although arranged marriages are still popular in many parts of our world, most of the people reading this book will have a choice in whom it is they decide to marry. That choice has with it the blessing of freedom, but it also carries with it the burden of responsibility. Marriage is a life-time covenant.

The traditional marriage vows that are typically heard at all weddings regardless of religious denomination or affiliation include questions like: "Will you promise to love him/her and honor him/

her in sickness and in health? Will you have and hold him/her from this day forward for better or for worse, for richer or for poorer and cherish one another until death separates you?"

Friend, those are serious promises we're making when we say "I will" to those questions. Unfortunately, many of those promises are broken and torn to shreds in court in less than 8 years by more than half of the people who make them. But regardless of how enthusiastically people dive into marriage and how quickly they leap out of it, vows are promises. A vow is my word. It represents my character and commitment. The question will come up time and time again in marriage. When things get difficult and adversity and disappointment are constant, will you and I keep our word?

In health of course, but what about in sickness? What about if our once healthy spouse becomes disabled in some way or another? What if they're confined to a wheelchair or they have some kind of medical trauma that leaves them a fraction of the person they once were? Will we love all of them that's left? Will we love her with one breast if cancer takes the other one? Will you love him with one leg if diabetes takes the other one? If post-traumatic stress disorder causes them to be less stable mentally and emotionally, will you still keep your vow?

For better of course, but what about when worse comes? Will you still love forever when her side of the family is now causing a lot of anxiety and pressure because of poor decisions made by her siblings? Will you remain committed when his now 15-year old has to move in with you all because he's been in constant trouble at school and with the law and now living with his father and your impressionable and curious 12-year old is his last resort? Is that the final straw for you or will you figure it out together?

For richer, for sure, but what about if poorer visits? What if the business that was once thriving and provided a stable living goes under, and the financial devastation left you living at a level of lack and poverty you never saw yourself experiencing?

RECOVERING FROM MARITAL INFIDELITY

These vows can take on even greater meaning when there's been unfaithfulness. For some, that's the unpardonable sin. For many however, when they look at all they've invested in their marriage, and all of the history that they have together, and the future that may still be hoped for together, they go through the arduous journey of trying to patch up the garment of their marriage that's now tattered into a thousand pieces. But where do you start?

Well here's some good news; most great marriages that I know, have experienced some kind of trauma that forced them to implement disciplines and habits to make the marriage great. It's not always a fidelity trauma, sometimes it's a financial trauma, or even a big fight that does it. Whatever it is, something shatters the relationship. The blessing that can come out of a catastrophic experience is the fact that it trebuchets the couple into a system of healthy marital habits that seek to not only avoid the antecedent suffering but to build a pleasant union. Quite frankly, many marriages would not improve without some kind of enormous difficulty that snapped the marriage out of its coma of normalcy and into a life-giving relationship.

So, where does the restoration begin? Counseling and account-ability are essential at this point. There's no way a couple can survive, much less recover, from such a devastating experience as infidelity without the help of competent allies.

There must be someone that the unfaithful spouse especially is 100% accountable and submitted to. That's partly because the "cheater" if you will, has been secretly living according to his/her own set of rules for a period of time. Now their life must not only be kept in the light of accountability but must be brought under the wisdom and authority of someone that has their best interest and the interest of their marriage and family. Being accountable is something the unfaithful spouse wasn't doing and actually has grown accustomed to not doing.

This accountability to a counselor, pastor, mentor, and their spouse is terribly important because breaking free from an affair is no small task. The intoxicating and sometimes deeply emotional connection that usually accompanies an affair is very difficult to walk away from.

Part of that "walking away" from the Side Chick or Side Slick means cutting off access and not allowing them to easily contact you. It means un-friending, un-following, and blocking the person on all

Social Media platforms. It often means changing your cell phone number. It could mean changing jobs or even relocating if necessary depending upon the closeness proximity-wise that you and the Side Chick have.

To not make deliberate moves to cut off access is a recipe for disaster because it's impossible to have been intimate with a person and not miss them from time to time. It is natural for us to reach out to people that we miss, so we have to protect ourselves from acting on that natural inclination.

Moving forward with your life and family requires some tough decisions that will cause you pain but will protect you and the Side Chick from future rendezvous. Changing contact information doesn't just protect you from contacting them, but it protects them from catching up with you. At a time when your marriage is in desperate need of rebuilding trust the last thing you need is a relapse due to not preventing access to yourself.

A lot of times people who are working to rebuild trust get discouraged when it seems like it's taking a long time. But keep in mind that whenever a building has been demolished, the cleanup and rebuilding process takes a lot longer than the demolition. One boulder of infidelity can knock the building down, but the building is rebuilt one brick at a time.

When speaking of what the process of rebuilding trust looks like in their book, "Worthy of Her Trust: What You Need to Do to Rebuild Sexual Integrity and Win Her Back", Stephen Arterburn and Jason B. Martinkus write, "It is long, arduous, messy, absolutely not formulaic, sometimes comical, often depressing, and always mysterious. It is a process of trial and error. Certainly, there are similarities in the way people experience rebuilding trust, but at the end of the day, the process is *your* process."[2]

Also, it's important to not just see yourself rebuilding trust if you've been the perpetrator of infidelity in your union, you have to also see yourself as rebuilding your entire self.

At the end of the day, cheating is always a character issue. And rebuilding our character takes a lot of time and attention. Indeed, not rebuilding our character after infidelity is a major problem because we can't remain the same person we were, and think that we won't end up doing the same things that we did. We must mature and become a better version of ourselves to not behave in the same way under the same circumstances.

Another way that we must Side Chick proof our marriages is by being able to handle something I talk about in my book, "A Second Chance: Grace for the Broken": The importance of handling euphoric recall and what I call emotional RSVPs back into your dark past.

When a person experiences euphoric recall regarding a past affair, it is a feeling of blissful memories of the infidelity. However, those thoughts aren't just full of pleasure but they're also filled with blind spots and hidden vices and traps.

No one can deny that what makes an affair so enticing is the incredible pleasure and thrills that are associated with having sneaky fun with somebody. And the temptation to revisit those pleasurable times may come with great frequency especially during the initial recovery period. Those tempting thoughts may periodically return for years to come. In fact, they may whisper to us for the rest of our lives. One of the secrets to handling those challenging times is not just to say no to them and resist them, but to add to those euphoric memories the danger, risk, hurt, pain, immaturity, recklessness, and costs of all of that fun. That's usually very sobering and it really requires a level of sober thinking to make good decisions.

KEEP MOVING ON TO THE NEXT THING (FORGIVENESS)

Back sometime in the early 1990s while serving on staff at the New Song Bible Fellowship Church in Lanham, MD, I was privileged to meet a couple whose influence still blesses me to this very day. I don't know if I've ever seen up close a more admirable, loving, and impressive marriage in my life than the marriage of Chris and Vanessa Moore.

They led the Married Couple's Ministry at New Song and as far as I know, they haven't written any books about marriage, and they don't have a podcast or television series on marriage, but without them, I don't know if Vicki and I would've made it through the first 5 years of our marriage.

I'd like to thank them for their example and how they made marriage look fun to me. I needed to see that because it gave me something to dream and hope for. One of the many things that I learned from them is the phrase, "Move on to the next thing." What that means is, make sure you don't get stuck in any arduous and difficult space in your marriage. View it as a journey that's always headed in a wonderful, growing direction, and when you hit a rough spot, forgive each other and move on to the next thing. That advice for me, though not always followed, has been priceless. I guess I owe them at least dinner for that.

Consistently moving on to the next thing is critical for the success of a marriage because you can't live life successfully going in reverse. Sometimes wishing things were the way they once were can keep us emotionally stuck and hoping for a day and time that will never return. Move on to the next thing, every day, throughout the day, as much as you can. Most things are not worth the derailment of progress that we allow them to cause.

This is easier said than done because when we are hurt or disappointed in our relationship, we experience either a fight, flight, or freeze reaction. We want to fight and argue because hurt people want to hurt people. We want to flee and create distance between ourselves and our mate to prevent further injury. Or we get emotionally stuck, freeze up, and find ourselves depressed and experiencing great difficulty moving forward. During these times what we need is God's help to set us free and grant us the liberty to move out of the bondage of our reaction to a disappointing moment and forgive and move on to the next thing.

This is so important because the reality is a marriage has no hope of progress without regular forgiveness. We have to extend and receive forgiveness frequently, because it's impossible to live in close proximity to another flawed human being every single day and not offend each other and rub each other wrong periodically. Forgiveness is essential, not just for something huge like infidelity, but for something smaller like, "You ate my dessert that I was looking forward to eating, that I thought I had safely hidden from you."

Forgiveness is also very important to strengthening and Side Chick-proofing our marriage because we all have things that trigger us and open up what I call our "files". In fact, we all have file cabinets in our minds and souls where we store emotional pain and trauma. Certain behaviors or actions or words or even the lack of words or actions from our spouse can trigger us and re-open those files.

So even though we're literally dealing with something in the moment, we're emotionally dealing with everything in the past that's attached to and activated by the moment. Sometimes the person who activated us gets discouraged because they feel like we keep bringing up the past; but actually, they brought up the past with a present behavior that reminded us of the past. It happens to all of us.

Forgiveness reduces the file and makes it less active in our relationship. However, it's important that we don't confuse the extension of forgiveness with the earning of trust. Those are not the same things, in fact, forgiveness is a gift. The word "give" sits right in the middle of the word "forgiveness", but in the middle of the word "trust" is "u" and that's because it's up to you to earn trust.

Forgiveness is compassion-based. Trust is character-based. Although we can be forgiven without changing, trusting us without changing would be foolish.

Again, I deal more extensively with this subject in messages and teachings on my website <u>www.sagacitycompany.com</u>.

MAKE A HEALTHY MARRIAGE THE GOAL

I'm actually typing this section of the book on a long flight from D.C. to Los Angeles where Vicki and I are headed to attend a wedding that I'm officiating. Unfortunately, we're not sitting together because our flights were booked separately. Meanwhile, the person that I'm sitting next to on the flight, whom I'm hopeful can't see what I'm about to write, has been coughing repeatedly throughout the flight. What's got me unnerved by it is the fact that she continues to cough without ever covering her mouth. So being the germophobe that I am, not only do I think that's rude and impolite, I also think it's disgusting. Nevertheless, not even my heavy sighs and squirms when she does it seems to matter. She continues…

But here's what I've got on my side in this situation. One is prayer. "Lord, please don't let this lady cause me to get sick." The other thing I have on my side is the fact that I have a relatively healthy lifestyle in which I exercise regularly, get plenty of rest, and I take lots of vitamin C on a daily basis. I'm actually fairly confident between my spiritual habit of prayer and my lifestyle and supplement habit, that even if she's sick, I'm going to be alright because I'm healthy enough to resist it.

You see, the truth is health prevents colds so the best way of avoiding a cold is to stay healthy. Likewise, the best way of avoiding a cold, sick marriage is to keep it warm and healthy.

Here are a few suggestions that Vicki and I use, and some that we are planning to use.

Pray together.

Deuteronomy 32:30 How could one person chase a thousand of them, and two people put ten thousand to flight, unless their Rock had sold them, unless the Lord had given them up?

I love that verse. Its context is a military war scene, where the writer is describing the incredible power that God provides the members of His army. So much power that one soldier could make a thousand enemies run in fear. Then it says that if there are two soldiers, together they could put 10,000 enemies to flight.

That's an amazing picture of the power of unity between two people who are fighting for the same cause. They can do ten times more together than they can apart.

I feel that way about my relationship with Vicki. God has allowed me to be effective without her, but my effectiveness is exponential with her. One of the most powerful ways that we connect together is through praying together every day.

Sadly, for the first 23 years of our marriage, we rarely prayed together. As powerful as daily prayer is between a couple, it's surprising to me how many couples that I'm privileged to speak to around the country pray alone every day, but don't pray with each other.

I plead with you for the health and well-being of your marriage to make daily prayer together a regular habit. Even when you're separated by distance due to travel or work, just call each other and pray. Even if it's just for 60 seconds, pray together for your children, your marriage, your health, your finances, your upcoming decisions, your parents, people that you know who need prayer, just pray together. It's a powerful tool.

In addition to this powerful spiritually-connecting habit, it would be great if the two of you could also worship God together as well. To join hands and hearts and minds in places of corporate worship like church, where you are spiritually trained and challenged together is also important. In fact, if you attend the same church, (which I think is ideal), and one or both of you volunteer or serve at your church, be careful that your service doesn't perpetually separate you from shared times of worshipping together. It's very important.

Play together. I say this repeatedly on my social media posts and in marriage counseling and talks that I give, "If you're not having fun, you're done." I don't mean that statement literally, but what I am absolutely sure of is how critically important fun is in a marriage.

With all of the things that are serious and challenging in our lives, including work, parenting, exercising, dieting, traffic, health challenges, difficult neighbors and family members, etc., we have to make our marriages one of the places that we find joy and contentment.

I suggest that you make it a habit to get away for a weekend, ideally once a quarter, and preferably without your children. Just getting away from your normal environment and going somewhere that you'd both enjoy can do wonders for your marriage.

I also suggest at least one extended trip or vacation a year without the kids and another one with the kids with each lasting for 5-10 days. It's critical. Go wherever your budget will allow and do whatever you can afford, but get away together and re-connect. You'd be amazed at how good it can feel to just be together without the regular responsibilities you have when you're home.

On a weekly basis, I suggest that a part of your playing together be going on a date. Every week, without compromise, (unless there's some emergency or something you can't get out of), make sure you date your mate. It's terribly important.

When you date, make sure you don't go out and talk about problems and challenges, save those conversations for more serious times. Let the date just be fun. I suggest that you rotate who plans the date each week, so that there's a mutual commitment not only to the time spent together, but also a mutual commitment invested in securing the childcare and planning the date as well. Surprise each other sometimes with something you know your spouse would love, like tickets to a concert to see his or her favorite artist. Or plan a surprise spa package for the two of you, or a dinner cruise and limousine service. The sky's the limit, but date your mate and celebrate your love for each other.

In order to consistently play together when you have young children, it is critical that you have baby sitters or child care support. By the way, people who do that work are angels sent from heaven who have saved more marriages and families than they'll ever know. To find somebody that you can trust with caring for your kids, especially if it's somebody that your kids actually like is a major blessing! I suggest you build a database of childcare supporters: grandparents, aunts, uncles, godparents, sitters from the church, friends, etc. Mix it up, because you've got a lot of dating and traveling to do.

Study together. Vicki and I haven't done this exercise regularly, but something that I hope we can add into our marital connection system soon is some time where we read books and articles together. We can allow our minds to collectively absorb material together, growing and learning together. Just the idea excites me, because my wife's mind is so profoundly brilliant, and her vocabulary is off the charts. Although she's socially quiet, I learn so much from her when she speaks and shares her thoughts. Hopefully you'll join us in your own marriage and read material that will help us all grow together as couples.

Eat meals together. Connecting around food has always been a popular way for people to relate. In fact, whenever someone is interested in getting acquainted with you, or catching up with you, they usually suggest doing it over coffee or a meal. The table is a powerfully connecting piece of furniture.

Recently I did a biblical study on the word "table" and I was amazed at how much the table meant in the Bible. It was the scene of deals made, communion, business meetings, military plans, nurturing conversations, welcome and hospitality, provision, and so much more. But most of all, it's a place of connection, because whenever people come to a table, the goal is to connect.

Therefore, I think it's important to have times when we have coffee or meals together that are not official dates but have powerful connecting potential. Use the table to check in and see how things are going with one another. How are projects and goals coming along? Find out if there's anything you can help with or pray for with your spouse. Make the table or even the kitchen counter, if suitable, a place of regular connecting.

Recline together. I know of couples who do something that they call "couch time". This is a time where they both relax on a sofa or love seat and just talk about their day. It's a time to decompress and express both the challenges and victories of the day. It's a time to reconfirm your love for and appreciation of each other and just to re-center the relationship in its proper place above every other human relationship, including the children. In fact, children should be taught to respect mom and dad's "couch time" and give them the space that they need to connect.

Get together financially. In Genesis 2:24 the Bible says that when a man gets married, he's supposed to leave his father and mother and be *joined* to his wife, and the two of them become one. Joined means one. If we're joined, then ideally everything financial should be joint -- joint savings accounts, joint tax returns, joint checking accounts, joint retirement accounts, joint goals, joint ownership.

Too many marriages have been structured in a way that is naturally divisive -- separate cell phone accounts, separate bank accounts. One person's responsible for certain bills and the other is responsible for others. It can become a discordant scenario really quickly, especially if there's immaturity and irresponsibility on the part of one or both spouses when it comes to finances. That can be an extremely alienating issue that bleeds into other areas of the marriage.

I recommend the most literal system of unity and accountability in the marriage financially, no matter which spouse makes the most or even all of the money. It's all ours! Either we're one or we're not. Regardless of how much money you have or earn, don't assume that because your spouse sincerely enjoys the lifestyle your money enables them to have means that they are only there for the money. The money for most is just a bonus.

The 10 Second Rule. The 10 Second Rule is something that I use with couples when I have them stand up and hold each other without words and try to let their hearts and souls connect through an embrace.

It's good to use when you can't stop arguing about something that at the end of the day is really not a big deal. It re-centers the relationship and reminds the two of you what matters most and that is each other.

Rarely is 10 seconds enough, so I always say to hold each other for at least 10 seconds, or let each person count slowly to 10. The point is, it's an intentional act of connection that disarms us and allows us to re-connect.

Affirmations. There are millions of people in the world who read daily affirmations to inspire and motivate themselves and shape their thinking for the day ahead. How cool and empowering it would be if there were daily affirmations that we said to and about our spouse? Praising them for their physical attractiveness, their spiritual disciplines, their wisdom, their love, their taste in clothing, their hairstyles, and on and on and on. We should be each other's biggest cheerleader. Cheering is not just for women, men need to celebrate and encourage their wives as well.

Into Me See (Intimacy). One of the greatest gifts that we can give each other is the gift of unconditional love. The kind of love that allows us to express the way that we feel about something good or bad, and not be punished or judged for it. Sharing our feelings with each other without attacking one another is so incredibly important to a healthy marriage. To know that I can not only have fun with my wife, but I can have fear and frustration in front of my wife and still have her respect and love is priceless. I don't have to hide from her and secretly take my deepest fears and feelings elsewhere.

We need to make room and opportunities in our marriage for each person to just share how they're honestly feeling. If they want feedback, we give it to them lovingly, but if they just want to vent and process things on their own, we respect that as well.

The goal is to focus on improving these individual areas so that we can improve the overall relationship and make it healthy.

Affirmations

I made a decision to marry my spouse and I made a promise to remain married to him/her until death separates us. I will keep my vow.

Rebuilding trust in marriage is a lot harder and takes a lot longer than it did to originally build and lose trust. I will consistently work to rebuild trust for the rest of my life.

I spoke at The First Baptist Church of Glenarden in Upper Marlboro, MD once and I shared a wedding vow analogy in my message. 61 seconds of that analogy was captured on video and posted on Facebook and at the time of my writing this book it's gotten over 7 million views. Here's the link if you'd like to see it - https://www.facebook.com/firstbaptistglenarden/videos/1603927296304163/

CHAPTER 12:

IN MARRIAGE, TOOLS ARE JUST AS IMPORTANT AS RULES

Obviously, there must be rules established to protect the fidelity of the marital union. There should be rules regarding what is appropriate and what is inappropriate social activity. There should be rules regarding travel itineraries and interactions. There should be rules regarding appropriate and inappropriate conversations with persons outside of the marriage. Rules are important because they create boundaries and limit unhealthy exposure in the relationship.

But the marriage also needs tools in order to be successful as well. Trying to fix something that needs repair or even trying to do maintenance work on something that needs tweaking requires the right tools.

MY FAVORITE TOOLS

Two of the most important tools that I've learned and developed over the years are what I call the SBI and the LUVAFA tools.

The first one I learned from my Pastor, John K. Jenkins, Sr. He pastors the First Baptist Church of Glenarden, the largest church in the entire state of Maryland. He teaches this tool as a conflict resolution method that can be used in all relationships. And the letters SBI stand for "Situation", "Behavior", and "Impact". This is how it works:

When there is hurt or disappointment that has you stuck as a couple, the offended spouse's job is to make a request for a conversation with their mate, and they should use the SBI tool.

They start with the particular *situation*, describing the setting, then they share the hurtful action, words, inaction, or silence (which represents the *behavior*) of the other person. Then they share what *impact* that behavior had on them.

Now the key to utilizing this tool is to try to limit the SBI to one situation because whenever you run off multiple situations that offended you to a person, they naturally feel overwhelmed and tend to get defensive instead of empathic.

It's also important to focus on the facts of the situation and the actual behavior and not try to suggest intent or motive on the part of the person, or to try to make a character judgment about the person. Just state what happened (behavior), when and where it happened (context/situation), and the way it made you feel as a result (the impact it had on you.).

Here's an example of a proper SBI.

Offended Spouse: Hi. May I speak with you about something when you have a few moments?

Offending Spouse: (Sigh). Ok. What would you like to discuss?

Offended Spouse: The other day, when we were riding in the car home from Michael's football practice, I was trying to listen to a conversation that Michael and his friend Anthony were having in the back of the car, and I reached to turn your radio down so that I could hear them, and you pushed my arm away and told me at the top of your voice to "stop trying to control everything. This is *my* car, and I listen to what I want to listen to in *my* car. When we're in *your* car, do I try to change the stations? No! I listen to your little church music even though that's not what I want to hear. When we're in *your* car, we listen to what *you* want to listen to, but we're in *my* car now, so *I* control the music in *this* car!"

Your push was kind of aggressive and I noticed the boys got quiet when you did it, so I chose not to tell you why I wanted the radio turned down because now they were listening to and watching us.

I even mumbled while you were yelling at me that I wasn't trying to change the station, but you didn't hear me and it was already a scene in the car. I didn't want to change the station, I just wanted to turn the music down, because I heard Anthony say something about his mom's health, and I know that she'd been worried about his feelings about it, so as a fellow mom, I wanted to hear how he was processing her cancer diagnosis and treatment and see if I could be of help or give her an update on how he was handling it.

I was hurt, first of all, because you physically pushed my arm away from the radio.

I was hurt secondly because you said I always try to run things and I'm not even sure what you meant.

I was hurt thirdly because those children saw you handle me that way.

Now before I give the proper response or the LUVAFA tool, let me tell you the incorrect way for the *previous* SBI to be expressed.

Offended Spouse: Hi. May I speak to you about something when you have time?

Offending Spouse: (Sigh). Ok. What would you like to talk about?

Offended Spouse: For the 18 years we've been together you have repeatedly treated me with disrespect. In fact, I remember the week before our wedding when you didn't even introduce me to your ex-girlfriend when we saw her at the mall. (Tears) I have had to live with your abuse, mistreatment, and meanness for 18 years and I'm tired.

You have put your hands on me. You have yelled at me repeatedly in front of our own son and you've even done it in front of other children for no reason! (Sobbing).

I've asked the women in my church to pray for me and for our marriage, but I don't know how much more I can take. For once, I would just like for you to treat me with respect and stop bullying me.

Offending Spouse: (Incredulously) When have I ever put my

hands on you? What are you talking about? If anything, you're the abuser around here! Why is that every time we have a conversation, you bring up everything from our past?

Offended Spouse: I bring all of that up because the other day, when we were riding home from Michael's football practice and his friend Anthony was in the car, you were acting mean that whole evening. It seems like you always have an attitude when it comes to going with me to Michael's football practice. Maybe you don't want to be seen with me or you don't want people to know that you are married. But every time we go to pick up Michael from practice together there's some kind of drama.

Offending Spouse: Drama? What drama?

Offended Spouse: Yes, drama. Anyway, Anthony and Michael were in the back seat and I heard Anthony say something to Michael about his mom's cancer diagnosis and treatment and I wanted to hear how he was processing that, and I can't believe that you didn't even care enough to turn down your music so that we could be there for this young boy. When I tried to turn the music down, you totally snapped. You practically broke my arm, you pushed it so hard. Then you started yelling at me in front of the boys at the top of your lungs about how controlling I am and how I am not going to run your car, and on and on you went for 10 minutes, berating me and tearing me down in front of those young boys. Is that how you want them to treat women? Like you treat me? If I wasn't so sad for them that they had to witness your behavior, I would've cried right in that car. But I know that's what you want, Mike. You like to hurt me and see me cry. You like to break me down and humiliate me. That makes you feel powerful, doesn't it?"

Do you see the difference? When you start loading up situations on a person, and you start analyzing their intentions and motives, and you get away from the specific situation, the specific behavior, and the specific impact it had on you, you're just on your way to a verbal brawl.

Here's how the Offending Spouse should respond to an appropriate SBI. He/she should use the LUVAFA tool which stands for "Listen", "Understand", "Validate", "Apologize", seek "Forgiveness", and make

"Amendments". Let me touch on each point before giving an example of this tool.

Everything starts with *listening*. Really listening. Make sure you don't miss anything and listen with the intent and goal of understanding. To *understand* someone requires humility because it means to stand under them and allow them to instruct you. You prove that you've truly listened to a person when you can tell them exactly what you understood them to be saying as they expressed themselves. In fact, because the person and the relationship are both so important to you, you're even willing to take it a step further by saying, "Using a percentage from 0 to 100%, how well do you think I understand what you've communicated to me?" And if they say anything less than 100% even if it's 95%, then ask them to help you understand the last 5%.

Once you've understood your offended mate, then it's very important to *validate* them by letting them know that they're not crazy for feeling the way that they do about your behavior or words and that if you were in their situation, you may have handled things a lot worse than they did.

Next, it's very important to own your stuff and *apologize* for the things you said, did, left undone, or unsaid that caused your loved one pain. In addition to apologizing, ask your mate if they can find it in their heart to *forgive* you for the wrong that you are truly sorry for doing.

But it's not enough to stop with an apology and request forgiveness because many people do that over and over and over again for the same things. The final step in this tool is to make *amendments* and to either suggest things that you are willing to do to prevent this pain from happening again or to ask your spouse what amendments they'd like you to make that you can agree upon. That's the LUVAFA tool. Here's how it should work when a proper SBI is given as in the example above. By the way, it doesn't have to flow in any particular order, but all 6 parts of the LUVAFA tool need to be a part of your response for healing to begin and progress to be made towards mending the relationship and moving forward.

Offending Spouse: First of all, Gail, I am so sorry for what I said and did to you. (Apology). I had no idea Anthony was talking about his mom's cancer. (Listening) I'm so sorry. (Apology) I really thought you were trying to control the radio, and I felt at the time like you were judging me because of the song that was playing. I was wrong. Please forgive me. (Seeking Forgiveness) Please forgive me as well for pushing your arm away. (Seeking Forgiveness) In hindsight, I remember it just being a reflex to stop you from getting to the radio, but it was still inappropriate and for that, I am so sorry as well. You were only trying to be there for Anthony and be a support for him and his mom through this difficult time. (Listening and Understanding). I can totally understand why my selfish response to you would be so hurtful. (Validation) I can't apologize enough, Honey. I am so sorry. (Apology) I'm not sure if I missed anything that you were trying to communicate to me about the situation, if so please let me know. (Making sure there's Understanding). And please tell me how you would like me to handle situations like this in the future so that you never have to go through this again. (Amendments)

Offended Spouse: (Relieved) Thank you for your apology and I forgive you. No, I wasn't trying to control you or judge you for your music. I'm sorry if it came across that way or if I've come across that way in the past. I actually like the music you listen to as well. I really just wanted to hear Anthony. So, thank you for understanding. You didn't leave anything out, you got it, thank you. As far as what I'd like for you to do in the future is just trust me if I reach to turn down your radio. Just know that it's not to judge you but I'm doing it for a good reason. I just want you to trust me and believe the best about me.

Offending Spouse: You've got it, Babe. Consider it done.

That felt so good to write that I hate to give the wrong way of responding to your spouse when they're hurt. However, it's important to see, read, and hear the wrong way as well, so that you'll be aware of it when it's happening.

Here's a typical response to an *improper* SBI:

Offending Spouse: *You* were hurt!? You!? What about me? How come you always get to be the victim in this marriage? How come you can do whatever the heck you want without any consequence, and I just have to suck it up and be humble and bite my tongue because the pastor says, "Happy wife, happy Life"?

I'm sick of it, Gail! I'm sick of how every time I stand up to your controlling ways, I get a correction talk 3 days later, after you shut me down sexually, by the way. Yeah, let's talk about that! Let's talk about how I have to go weeks at a time without having any intimacy with my own wife, because I don't dot every freaking "I" and cross every darn "T". How about that Sister Gail!? Let's talk about that!

And you're talking about abuse!? Ha ha ha! That's funny. Where should I start? Should I start with the day you threw my cell phone at me and cut my head? (Pointing to his head) Scars don't go away Gail.

Or wait a minute, how about the time you locked me out of my own bedroom and I had to sleep on the couch in my work clothes in front of our son because you were mad at me for not paying a stupid bill on time!

But you know what, I'm not going to even go down memory lane. That's your specialty. But in response to your little comment about if that's how I want those boys to see how to treat a woman. What you should be asking is what kind of woman do you want to portray in front of them. The kind that tries to control, judges, and disrespects her husband in front of her kids and treats him like a kid, telling him what he can and cannot listen to on the radio. I'm a grown man, Gail!

Here's the deal folks. The reason why the SBI tool is so critical for the offended spouse, and the LUVAFA tool is so important for the offending spouse is because without them those bad examples that I gave above will become the norm. Relationships that handle conflict and disagreement this way, are sure to be painful and hopeless.

I've been married to Vicki now for 3 decades and I can honestly say that the majority of our marriage was miserable. That's not an understatement. For 23 years we had mostly bad years. It was sad, lonely, sometimes hostile and volatile, and sometimes cold and scary. The only thing that kept us together was our stubborn commitment to God and to our vows. Furthermore, neither of us wanted to hurt our children or our church family by divorcing. So, for years we just survived. What I've been sharing with you in this book are the things we started doing on a regular basis that miraculously turned a miserable marriage into one that we both enjoy.

Another tool that I use that I've found to be really helpful for married couples is what I call a Marriage Quality Measurement Grid. In Chapter 11, I talked about the importance of making your marriage healthy. The Marriage Quality Measurement Grid tool that I developed and use when I speak to or counsel couples can help. I'd like to share it with you here.

THE MARRIAGE QUALITY MEASUREMENT GRID

SAMPLE

	WHERE WOULD YOU SAY YOUR MARRIAGE IS RIGHT NOW?	WHEN THINGS WERE THE VERY WORST IN YOUR MARRIAGE. And how BAD was it?	WHEN THINGS WERE THE VERY BEST IN YOUR MARRIAGE. And how GREAT was it?
SOLID — AMAZING			
GREAT			✳ 2005 Hawaii Trip
VERY GOOD			
GOOD			
SHAKY — ABOVE AVERAGE			
OK			
DANGEROUS — STRUGGLING	✳ TODAY		
BAD			
VERY BAD			
TERRIBLE		✳ 2011 Text Messages and Emails	
HOPELESS			

Now using the Grid, place an asterisk where you would describe your marriage is today. If it's spot on one of the words, put the asterisk to the right of the word. If it's between two of the words, place the asterisk in between and to the right of those two words. For me, based on a recent inquiry with Vicki, right now, my marriage is somewhere between Very Good and Great. That's not perfect, but it's a long way from where it once was. By the way, women typically don't rank the marriage as high as men, unless they feel really secure in the marriage emotionally and financially. Men usually place their ranking higher after they've had sex and dinner cooked for them, than at times when nothing's cooking in the kitchen or the bedroom.

Now imagine that Amazing would be a 10. Great is a 9. Very Good is an 8. And Good is a 7. Anything from Good to Amazing or 7-10 is solid. Your marriage is Green.

Anything from Above Average to Ok is shaky and the marriage is in the Yellow range at a score of a 5-6.

Finally, anything from Struggling to Hopeless is dangerous and in the red zone with a score of 0-4. That also usually means a lot of things are probably happening to cope with the pain of the marriage that may be keeping it unhealthy or making it even worse.

I have couples do this exercise to get a feel for where their marriage is, not to discourage them or to get them over-confident, but to give them a goal for their marriage's improvement. Because as I'll show you in a moment, even if your marriage is currently "Amazing" it is in constant need of improvement and maintenance because that can all change in a moment.

In fact, without doing anything good or bad, a marriage can drop down one level, just because of apathy and disengagement. Just being neutral with each other will take the quality of the relationship down. That's because marriage is a naturally atrophying relationship and much of the stuff in our lives pulls us apart rather than pushes us together. Busy schedules, professional responsibilities, parental duties, bill payments and budgeting, calendar planning, working out, extended family, church work, community involvement, higher learning, and on and on the list goes of things that move us from intimacy to strangers.

God forbid if there's a disappointment or disagreement or hurt in the relationship; it can drop down two levels in a matter of minutes, meaning a marriage can descend in quality from "above average" to "struggling" or from "ok" to "bad" really quickly. Which is why, if there's not a systemic effort and plan in place for the constant improvement of the marriage, then your marriage can be miserably clinging in an abyss for years.

Here's the second thing I want you to do with this tool. In the middle section of the Grid, I want you to place an asterisk in the space that represents where your marriage was at its worst and when. Include the time frame when your marriage was at its rock bottom. How bad did it get? When was it that bad?

Personally, our marriage remained somewhere between terrible and hopeless for years. In fact, hitting the ok level during that time felt like an oasis in a desert for us.

The reason why I have couples do this is because if there was a time when your marriage was in a more difficult place than it is now, then you've already experienced progress. More progress is possible, even probable if you work the strategies given in this book.

There's one more thing I want you to do with this tool and that is, I want you to write an asterisk on the right side of the Grid that describes a period when your marriage was at it's very best, and include the time period as well. For example, it may have been around Valentine's Day 3 years ago, or 8 summers ago. How wonderful was it, and when was it its very best? Or it may be that your marriage is at its very best now.

Now remember, wherever your marriage is at any time on the Marriage Quality Measurement Grid, it can drop down a level just with apathy and inactivity. Nothing bad has to happen, just being too busy to connect with each other will do it.

But it's also important to remember that one bad day can drop it two levels if something hurtful comes. Again, what I've come to understand is that in marriage, the quality of the relationship never goes up naturally. It only goes up with intentional, strategic, and effective effort. We have to swim upstream and intentionally to have a solid marriage.

Affirmations

I will study, practice, and work hard to master the SBI and LUVAFA tools so that my marriage will be effective at resolving conflict and recovering from hurt and disappointment.

Knowing that my marriage relationship will naturally drift apart, I will make regular investments into the quality and improvement of my marriage to make it progressively better.

CHAPTER 13:

MAKE YOUR OWN MARRIAGE FIRE

[15] Drink water from your own well—
share your love only with your wife.[a]
[16] Why spill the water of your springs in the streets,
having sex with just anyone?[b]
[17] You should reserve it for yourselves.
Never share it with strangers.
[18] Let your wife be a fountain of blessing for you.
Rejoice in the wife of your youth.
[19] She is a loving deer, a graceful doe.
Let her breasts satisfy you always.
May you always be captivated by her love.
[20] Why be captivated, my son, by an immoral woman,
or fondle the breasts of a promiscuous woman?[1]

This passage of Proverbs 5 is intended to protect marriages. I echo the words of verse 19 to every husband, "… Let (your wife's) breasts satisfy you *always*. May you *always* be captivated by her love." (Emphasis mine.)

Folks, sex is not some dirty, nasty thing. It is something powerful, explosive, pleasurable, connecting, and beautiful that was designed by God for marriage. It's only dark and dirty when it's done outside of the marriage relationship.

God made marital sex to be fun. It's one of the most pleasurable things that a human being can experience. The hormonal and adrenaline rush that we experience before and during sex, and the incredible state of relaxation afterwards, is unparalleled.

God also made marital sex to be a passionate experience. The erotic intensity of foreplay and sexual intercourse is a stress relieving gift to us.

Marital sex should also be creative. Having sex the same way, in the same location, and the same position, can become monotonous and uninteresting.

Sex in marriage was meant to be something that happened frequently. In fact, here's what the Bible says about this very subject in 1 Corinthians 7:

> *¹Now regarding the questions you asked in your letter. Yes, it is good to abstain from sexual relations.*
> *² But because there is so much sexual immorality, each man should have his own wife, and each woman should have her own husband.*
> *³ The husband should fulfill his wife's sexual needs, and the wife should fulfill her husband's needs.*
> *⁴ The wife gives authority over her body to her husband, and the husband gives authority over his body to his wife.*
> *⁵ Do not deprive each other of sexual relations, unless you both agree to refrain from sexual intimacy for a limited time so you can give yourselves more completely to prayer. Afterward, you should come together again so that Satan won't be able to tempt you because of your lack of self-control.²*

Clearly, in marriage, we should be having sex regularly. The regularity of sex should only be amended when there is mutual agreement to abstain temporarily for spiritual growth or physical health reasons. But even after the respite, we are instructed to resume regular sexual activity.

Marital sex should be connecting. It's not just about the pleasure of sex, it's about connecting with the person to whom I've committed my life and love to.

I'm not a professed "Sexpert", but I also believe that our sexual relationship in marriage should erotically engage all five senses -

Feeling, Tasting, Seeing, Hearing, Smelling. I see each of these senses engaged in the intimate relationship between Solomon and his Bride, the Shulamite Woman as recorded in the Song of Solomon.

Let him kiss me with the kisses of his mouth—
for your love is more delightful than wine.[3]

Here the Bride says, "Let him kiss me with the kisses of his mouth…" but she doesn't say let him kiss me on my mouth. Just let his lips go to work on me.

How pleasing is your fragrance;
your name is like the spreading fragrance of scented oils.
No wonder all the young women love you![4]

Here the Bride praises her man for how good he smells. Paying attention to our hygiene is important in our marital intimacy. Halitosis and body odor can be a major turn off sexually. Make sure you're fresh and clean when it's time for love-making especially, and make sure that what you think smells good is something that your spouse enjoys smelling.

Not only is the man fresh and clean in this story, but the Bride's fragrance is also pleasing to her man.

The king is lying on his couch,
enchanted by the fragrance of my perfume.[5]

Ladies, your fragrance should cause enchantment, not a distraction.

The verbal expression of love and appreciation between Solomon and his Bride are also great examples for us to follow as married couples. Notice how they both praise each other:

[2] *Like a lily among thistles*
is my darling among young women.
[3] *Like the finest apple tree in the orchard*
is my lover among other young men.
I sit in his delightful shade
and taste his delicious fruit.

⁴ He escorts me to the banquet hall;
it's obvious how much he loves me.⁶

One of the cool things about this particular section of their narrative is the fact that they are actually praising each other to others. That's huge. Speak well of your spouse before others, even when your spouse is not around. Most of the people in my life know the love that I have for Vicki because I always bring her up and broadcast my love and appreciation for her. I post about her on social media often. When I'm traveling, I bring her up in conversations with the person that's traveling next to me, especially if it's a woman that I don't know. It's a way of creating protective boundaries around my relationship and its fidelity.

Anyway, back to making our marriages fire.

Song of Solomon 2:6 says,

His left arm is under my head,
and his right arm embraces me.⁷

Now please picture this romantic love scene. Imagine Solomon holding his Bride with his left arm under her head, and his right arm embracing and holding her. That's a picture of intimate connecting. Good sex should involve this kind of pre-intercourse connecting. There shouldn't just be a rushing in for the kill, but a time of tender connecting and loving embrace, a time to express appreciation for one another and how grateful you are for the time you are currently sharing together. It's a time to appreciate and thank each other for taking the time to not just be together physically but to be emotionally present for this special time.

And that connection should continue during intercourse. Intercourse is not a time to check out, disconnect from each other and "do me", and satisfy myself. It's a time for both persons to stay in contact with each other not just physically but emotionally as well.

Finally, when the intercourse comes to a climatic end with orgasm, it is important to remain connected even then with embracing, cuddling, and appreciation. And, of course, a nap for us fellas.

Herein lies a key difference between marital sex and non-marital sex, for Christian men especially. Whenever a man whose moral convictions and religious beliefs inform him that having a sexual encounter with someone other than his wife is wrong, if and when he crosses that line, the shame he feels afterwards is as intense as the passion and desire he felt beforehand. His primary objective at that moment is not to cuddle and connect, but to get dressed and get away from the person he's crossed the line with.

Which is exactly why when a man is with his wife, he should make sure he stays connected to her even after climaxing and before he starts snoring, because there's no need to run away in shame.

Another way we learn to make our marriages fire from this awesome Book of the Song of Solomon is found in

Song of Solomon 2:13:

"The fig trees are forming young fruit,
and the fragrant grapevines are blossoming.
Rise up, my darling!
Come away with me, my fair one!"[8]

Solomon is inviting his beloved to get away with him to enjoy a rendezvous together. I can't tell you how important it is for married couples to get away periodically. In fact, I would suggest a minimum of 4 quarterly weekend getaways of 2-3 days each per year. Find the money and make it work. Your marriage needs it and deserves it.

Get away from the kids, especially. Get away from work, church, community service, laundry, dishes, cooking, yard work, and everything else, and just get away with each other to connect or re-connect. It's amazing!

Now if your marriage is in such a painful place that getting away doesn't appeal to either of you, I can relate. There was a time that Vicki and I were in such a bad place relationally that we didn't really want to go anywhere alone. It just reminded us of just how bad our relationship really was.

However, what did help was if we went out with or went away

with other couples and got to be around people whose marriages were at different levels of functionality and success. Group dating, or just going to the movies together allowed us to get away into environments where we didn't have to have one-on-one conversations with each other that would be cold or fiery and painful.

I say this to you because it's still important to get out together because, without any opportunities for fun and laughter and entertainment, the marriage is sure to continue to dissipate. Furthermore, you never know when being out with another couple might lead to a conversation that might give you all the light and hope that you need to begin to see change in your marriage.

I'm grateful that now, I'd rather be alone with Vicki than to go out with other couples. I just love her company, but sometimes we need to be connected to others and there are still times when we hit our rough spots where we'll have some quiet movie dates because things aren't clicking for us. The key is to consistently get out and get away.

Another fire producer in marriage is found in Song of Solomon 2:16-17:

> [16] My lover is mine, and I am his.
> He browses among the lilies.
> [17] Before the dawn breezes blow
> and the night shadows flee,
> return to me, my love, like a gazelle
> or a young stag on the rugged mountains.[9]

One thing that's so obvious in this erotic and romantic relationship is how verbally passionate they were to one another. Couples should consider role-playing the couple in the Book of Song of Solomon. Getting a modern translation of the Bible, and just reading and acting out the lines. Who knows, things may get hot.

In fact, Ladies, if you say to your husband in bed one night while you're barely clothed or not clothed at all, "Honey, you are mine, and I am yours. I want you to browse among the lilies tonight. I want you to be like a gazelle or a young stag on the rugged mountains tonight." I'll promise you, tears of joy will stream down his face.

This couple's sexual intimacy was awesome, but they also had something that was just as important. Notice what it says in Song of Solomon 4:9:

> *You have captured my heart,*
> *my treasure, my bride.*
> *You hold it hostage with one glance of your eyes,*
> *with a single jewel of your necklace.*[10]

Emotional closeness is one of the greatest treasures of a human to human relationship. "You have captured my heart." In fact, I'll dare say, that may be *the* most dangerous thing about an affair. It's not just sex between two people, because it's possible to have a sexual relationship with someone that you don't have an emotional closeness to. One of the most dangerous risks about an affair is if somewhere along the line, someone captures your heart. That's hard to recover from.

This is why it's so important that couples work on emotional closeness in their marriage relationship.

The fire heats up as we continue in the fourth chapter of the Song of Solomon. Fasten your seat belts for Song of Solomon 4:11-16:

> [11] *Your lips are as sweet as nectar, my bride.*
> *Honey and milk are under your tongue.*
> *Your clothes are scented*
> *like the cedars of Lebanon.*
> [12] *You are my private garden, my treasure, my bride,*
> *a secluded spring, a hidden fountain.*
> [13] *Your thighs shelter a paradise of pomegranates*
> *with rare spices—*
> *henna with nard,*
> [14] *nard and saffron,*
> *fragrant calamus and cinnamon,*
> *with all the trees of frankincense, myrrh, and aloes,*
> *and every other lovely spice.*
> [15] *You are a garden fountain,*
> *a well of fresh water*
> *streaming down from Lebanon's mountains.*
>
> **Young Woman**
> [16] *Awake, north wind!*

Rise up, south wind!
Blow on my garden
and spread its fragrance all around.
Come into your garden, my love;
taste its finest fruits.[11]

When the Bible says the power of death and life are in the power of the tongue, it's referencing how powerful our words can be. The tongue may be the most powerful body part in our marriages because of its power to speak words of praise and adoration and fidelity and romance to each other. It's also powerful because of the pleasure the tongue can give to our mates when we use it to titillate them.

Notice how erotic and passionate their kissing is in verse 11, so much so that Solomon describes what his Bride's lips taste like and what under her tongue tastes like.

Then he commences to move from her mouth and tongue to the smell of her clothes and down her body until he's describing her thighs in verse 13. There he stops and begins to describe her as a garden fountain, and a well of water streaming down from the mountain of Lebanon in verse 15. If you're still wondering what part of her body he's looking at and describing, listen to her response in verse 16, "come into your garden my love, and taste its finest fruits."

I bet some of y'all didn't know *that* was in the Bible! In fact, some of you have already gone to look it up to see if I'm making all of this up.

Let me cool things off a bit by showing how powerful the tongue or mouth is in marriage in another way as we see in Song of Solomon 1:15-16:

Young Man
[15] *How beautiful you are, my darling,*
how beautiful!
Your eyes are like doves.
Young Woman
[16] *You are so handsome, my love,*
pleasing beyond words!
The soft grass is our bed;[12]

Here we see how they each use the power of their tongues and mouths to give emotional pleasure to each other through words of affirmation. Let me ask you a question right here: Is there any person on the face of this earth, whose compliment of our appearance is more important than our spouse's? Of course not. That's why it's imperative that we don't leave it to others to tell our spouses how good they look, or how nice their outfits are, or how good their hair looks, etc. As the saying goes, "Charity begins at home." Be the first to acknowledge your spouse's beauty and attractiveness and be the one who makes the biggest deal about it.

Speaking of physical attraction, notice what King Solomon says regarding his Bride in Song of Solomon 7:1:

> *How beautiful are your sandaled feet,*
> *O queenly maiden.*
> *Your rounded thighs are like jewels,*
> *the work of a skilled craftsman.*[13]

Solomon says to his Beloved, "How beautiful are your '*sandaled*' feet." (Emphasis mine.) It may or may not come as a surprise to ladies, that men pay attention to a lady's feet. I want you ladies to know that all of the time and effort you spend getting pedicures is not in vain. The guys are watching.

Here's one more fire producer that I'd like to share from the Song of Solomon 7:10-13:

> [10] *I am my lover's,*
> *and he claims me as his own.*
> [11] *Come, my love, let us go out to the fields*
> *and spend the night among the wildflowers.*
> [12] *Let us get up early and go to the vineyards*
> *to see if the grapevines have budded,*
> *if the blossoms have opened,*
> *and if the pomegranates have bloomed.*
> *There I will give you my love.*
> [13] *There the mandrakes give off their fragrance,*
> *and the finest fruits are at our door,*
> *new delights as well as old,*

which I have saved for you, my lover.[14]

This time it is the wife that plans the getaway. I love it. Getaways should be important enough to both the husband and the wife, that both would take turns and time planning them.

And she's not just telling her man to get away with her so that they can go sightseeing and enjoy fine dining at new restaurants, which is all fine and dandy. What she clearly is planning for this getaway is some time for love-making with him. She says, "come away with me" and the place she describes is outdoors, and she says, "There, I will give you my love." I love it!

That's versatility and variety. Love-making shouldn't always be predictable. Be creative. Change locations, change positions, change who initiates and make it fun.

She basically tells him that "I'm going to hit you with something old and new. I'm going to give you what I know you like already, then I'm going to give you something that I know you've been wanting." (Excuse me if my imagination is getting away from me here.)

Folks, sex really matters in marriage. If you're having a disappointing, empty, sad sexual relationship in your marriage, just know that God didn't intend for it to be that way. He wants you to have a great sexual relationship in your marriage and of course it doesn't start in the bedroom, but it certainly ends there. (I'll say more about how what happens *in* the bedroom is impacted by what happens outside of the bedroom in the next chapter.)

Here are some things to keep in mind or consider that might be helpful.

If there is frustration over pre-mature ejaculation in marriage, one of the things to keep in mind is the fact that frequency usually produces stamina. Repetition also builds confidence. Conversely, if you're only having sex once or twice a month or less, the inconsistency makes prolonged intercourse arduous.

Also, if you're a man that's struggling with maintaining an erection, then research what you need to do to help in that area.

Seek medical advice and intervention if necessary. In fact, getting a quality executive physical that helps to identify hormone and vitamin deficiency can be very helpful. Also, wearing a condom might also be helpful in extending your erection.

It's also important, ladies, that you encourage your husband verbally during your sexual times and not wound him verbally or with your body language if his "performance" is less than stellar. Keep encouraging him.

A lot of men are addicted to pornography because the person on the screen doesn't judge them. I'm not saying that the behavior is justified, I'm just stating that men will run from the criticism and possible failure of pleasing their wives to self-pleasure if they don't feel emotionally safe.

Affirmations

I will honor my spouse even in their absence by mentioning them positively in conversations with others.

I will use my tongue to bring verbal appreciation and sensual pleasure to my spouse.

CHAPTER 14:

FALLING IN LOVE AGAIN

When you read through the Book of the Song of Solomon, it's fair to conclude that the man and woman focused on in that story were what we would call, "in love". Being in love is a beautiful thing. It's full of euphoric emotions and enchanted thoughts. It's a feel-good high like no other.

Do you remember what it was like to fall in love? Remember talking on the phone all night long until you had nothing else to say, and you'd start saying silly stuff like, "What are you doing right now?" (Rolling over in your bed to the other side) "I'm on the phone with you." (Back to the other side) "I mean, what else are you doing?" (Back to the other side) "Looking at your picture and the card you gave me. You're so sweet." (Back to the other side) You're pumping your fist like Tiger Woods, "Yeah, you like that card." (Back to the other side) "I don't like it, I love it…" (Back to the other side) "Do you sleep on your side or your back?"

If those conversations were ever recorded you'd be embarrassed to listen to them because of how jejune they were. Think about it, there you are lying in bed at 2:30 a.m. You have to get up for school in 4 hours, or you have to get up and prepare for work in like 3 hours and 30 minutes and the two of you are on the phone talking like two 8th Graders. Remember that?

Remember when you couldn't keep your hands off of each other, when hugging, cuddling and affection were regular parts of your relationship?

Remember when you would forget where you were when you were out at a restaurant tickling each other and making each other laugh? It didn't even matter to either of you that people at other tables were getting annoyed by your callow behavior.

Remember when y'all used to surprise each other all the time, and date all the time, and kiss all the time, and laugh all the time, and talk about future dreams all the time, and had fun all the time?

Remember when y'all played in the snow together and made snow angels and threw snow on each other and fell in the snow together and kissed and said to each other, "I've never been happier a day in my life?"

Then you got married... And over the years you've had children, then bills started piling up, and responsibilities, and commitments outside of the home, and the pressure of life and the real world started invading your love world. The marriage began to slowly grow distant and conversations became fewer and farther between each other.

It's not like you started hating each other, but the reality is, you both were just too exhausted to connect with each other. And the person that you once wanted to spend every waking moment of the day with is now just your husband or just your wife. This person that once seemed so amazing, now seems so normal. The magic is gone.

My therapist, Barry Levy[1] says that generally speaking, couples go through three phases in their relationship:

1. The Sight Moment. (Physical Attraction or Love at First Sight as it's often called.) Although a woman may be attracted to a man the moment she first sees him, it's a whole different level with a man when he finds a woman attractive. Believe it or not, men typically fall in love first, and it's because we're so visually oriented. When we see a woman, if we think she's hot, we feel that way in about 5 milliseconds, and that's not an exaggeration. Moreover, at the Sight Moment, a man is

paralyzed. In fact, a lot of men have had car accidents, bicycle accidents, walking accidents, etc., just by being paralyzed by a woman whose beauty captures them. Good thing women can't walk on clouds. There'd be plane crashes galore!

As men, during the Sight Moment, we've been hit in the face with basketballs, lost our spot in lines, fell off of gym equipment, been hit by cars, and sadly, even confronted by our wives when the Sight Moment has us staring at someone other than our brides. There's a part of the male brain that responds to pulchritude faster than it responds to danger. It's amazing how God has made us. (smile).

2. Next, we move from the Sight Moment to the <u>Knowledge Phase.</u> If the two people exchange contact information, and begin to get to know each other, then they add information to support and accelerate their fall into romantic bliss. In fact, because of today's technology, even before there's any personal contact made between each other, an aggressive search of the Internet commences as we scour for pictures, bios, history, beliefs, philosophies, employment, hobbies, children, and relationships. On and on the research goes on this person that we were smitten by at the Sight Moment. Also, during the Knowledge Phase, we typically discover the more unseemly things about the person and we have to determine if that information is pardonable or not.

3. If things continue to progress through the Knowledge Phase of the relationship, they move into the <u>Commitment Period.</u> This is when the two persons are tethered to each other in a commitment that says, "We're exclusive. I'm yours, you're mine."

Typically, it's somewhere during the Commitment Period that couples decide to spend the rest of their lives together, (although there are times when people impetuously elope prior to really evaluating who and what they're actually committing to.) This is so important because if there is one thing that has to be present in order to sustain a marriage throughout every single season it will experience, it is commitment. Commitment is absolutely essential to the perpetuity of a marriage.

Nevertheless, although commitment is very important when it comes to maintaining a marriage, I'm also convinced that the love that was once experienced doesn't have to be gone forever. Two people who were once in love, can fall in love again.

I think that's important to know and to believe because my guess is, if you've gone through the trauma of infidelity in your marriage, it may be difficult to remember how much you and your spouse were once in love. But rarely do two people make it to a courthouse, church, cruise-ship, or Caribbean Island to exchange wedding vows without first being in love with each other.

Yet, the brutish impact of an affair on a marriage disposes the relationship to something far less than ecstatic. In fact, even before an inappropriate, extra-marital relationship comes into play, oftentimes the married couple has fallen out of love with each other.

As I pen the last chapter of this book, I write from personal experience that your marriage can go from hopeless and terrible for years to a place where you can actually fall in love, again. What I'm about to tell you is not make-believe, but it's based on workable steps and practices.

WHY WE TEND TO FALL OUT OF LOVE

Before I cover how to fall in love *again*, I'll mention here some of the additional reasons why people fall out of love with each other. Keep in mind this is more of a representative list and not an exhaustive list.

1. *A Lack of Mutual Respect* causes us to fall out of love. Respect is one of those marital components that must be present for love to flourish. Unfortunately, there are times, when for a plethora of reasons, the wife doesn't show the kind of respect for her husband that he desires, and there are times when the opposite is true as well. In fact, disrespect for women from men is almost an inveterate behavior. Quite frankly, there are a lot of us men, who ignorantly view our wives as less than us in so many areas, and therefore we don't respect or value their

opinion or feelings. In fact, marriage expert and author John Gottman wrote the following statement in his blog quoting Jeff Pincus: *"Men who allow their wives to influence them have happier marriages and are less likely to divorce."*[2]

Gottman goes on to quote Kyle Benson who says, *"(Women) let their husbands influence their decision making by taking their opinions and feelings into account... the data also suggests that men do not typically return the favor."*[3]

Now here's the deep part, *"Statistically speaking, Dr. Gottman's research shows there is an 81% chance that a marriage will self-implode when a man is unwilling to share power."*[4]

Mutual respect can strengthen the love connection when it's present, and dissolve it when it's absent.

2. Another reason why couples tend to fall out of love is because of *a Lack of Emotional Intelligence*. The ability to be aware of various emotional signs and moments in a relationship and to be sensitive to those emotional signs and moments and to make the necessary adjustments is very important in a relationship that brings people as close for as long as a marriage does. For example, if you're having a great time with friends making jokes about your spouse, and your spouse is displaying uneasiness with the situation, continuing your comedic diatribe with the preface, "What's wrong Sam? You can't take a joke? Come on, lighten up, we're just having a few laughs," is sure to cost your marriage severely. By nature, we as men are usually not as emotionally intelligent and aware as women, and that's evident from the time we are children.

For example, when young boys play games, their focus is on winning, not their emotions or those of the others that are playing. They're not concerned about how they feel or about the feelings of other people participating in the game. They just want to win, even if it's not an organized competition with officials present. In fact, if one of the boys gets hurt during the game, the other boys will stand over him to see how serious it is, and pause just long enough to remove him from the court or field. Then he's immediately replaced by another player, or the other team must drop one of their players. But the focus is not on the injured boy or how he's feeling, the focus is still on the game. That's how we guys roll. It's not that we absolutely don't care about our injured comrade. In fact, we're all collectively saying to him as we resume play, "Hey, Bro, make sure you ice that when you get home. And tie that shoe up tight, man." But we're back to the game, and focused again on winning.

Conversely, when girls play games, unless it's an organized team sport, feelings are far more important than winning. In fact, if a group of girls are playing a game, and one of the girls simply tears up and stops playing and says, "We're not friends anymore," the whole game stops! She doesn't even have to be physically injured. No sprain. No broken bones. Just hurt feelings, and both teams discontinue any further competitive action. It's amazing!

"Kecia, what's wrong?" the entire group says. Meanwhile, the ball is just lying there on the court while all the girls are huddled around this emotionally-wounded girl trying to find out what's going on.

Ladies, with all due respect, that would *never* happen in a boy's or men's game. In fact, if a guy gets physically hurt during competition and he's unable to even move any of his limbs, before we even check on him, we first verify who had possession of the ball when the injury took place. I promise you that we're saying, "It's our ball and we're up two when we check it back up." In fact, the whole time we're standing over the injured player, waiting on him to muster enough strength to get out of the field of play, we're periodically saying to each other, "It's ya'll's ball and y'all are up two" so that no one forgets. Facts!

Now here's the major difference that I think follows us the rest of our lives, even into marriage. If a boy gets hurt, he's taken to the sideline and the game continues whether he's able to play again or not. Someone will yell out, "Sub!" That is an abbreviation for substitute, which means we need a healthy body to come in to replace the injured player. Once we clarify to the new player whose team he's on, the game resumes and we really aren't even thinking about the guy that got hurt.

But if a girl is hurt even emotionally during the game, the game not only stops, but here's the deep part, the game will not resume again at all until the two girls make up and the breach in the relationship is reconciled. Amazing!

It's like we're from two different worlds! What Dr. Gottman generally says about this is the fact that the way girls approach games, offers far better preparation for marriage and family life because they focus on relationships.[5]

This is very important. The most astute person in a relationship, from an emotional intelligence stand-point is usually the woman. She has natural inclinations toward being relational. If a marriage is going to have what my wife Vicki calls "emotional safety", there must be a competent level of mutual emotional intelligence. Gottman says that "Only 35% of men are emotionally intelligent."[6] Therefore, because this is a needed attribute for a healthy relationship, and it doesn't come naturally for a man like it does for most women, then this is something that a man has got to trust his wife to provide for him and educate him in.

In fact, I'd go so far to say that emotional disconnection is the foundation for just about every single problem in a marriage relationship. When a man is not naturally emotionally aware and intelligent, then becoming emotionally aware and intelligent will be like using your weak hand to write with and brush your hair and teeth with. Awkward, but doable and easier over time.

3. Another reason why we fall out of love in marriage is because *the Bed is Dead*. When the bed becomes just a place where we sleep and not a place where we have regular times of intimate connections, falling out of love is inevitable. This reason for people falling out of love is often connected to the previous

reasons, a lack of emotional intelligence, and a lack of mutual respect.

Generally speaking, men and women are often very different sexually. For example, in order for a woman to have sex, she must open up herself and let a man inside of her. It's more than just hormonal for a woman; it's deeply intimate, because she's letting someone in. That's why you ladies should stop saying you're going to give him "some" or not give him "some". Your body is not a dispenser. When you have sex with a man, you are letting him inside of you and that's deeply personal and demands a level of trust and love to give that kind of access.

That's why when a woman doesn't feel loved and treasured or respected and honored, and she doesn't feel that her feelings matter to her husband, she's emotionally closed to him. It's hard for her to open her legs when her heart is closed, because a woman's womb and her heart are impalpably connected. On the other hand, sex is not as emotionally deep for a man. The vertex of sex for a man is pleasure not necessarily intimacy.

Oftentimes the bed is dead because of how the relationship is going outside of the bed. Some couples make the mistake of trying to fix the bed, in the bed. They are thinking that bringing toys and videos and outfits to the bed is going to fix the bed. When the reality is, a dead bed is the fruit that grows from the root of a lack of respect and emotional connection that happens throughout the day. Cutting the lights out is not going to make us forget how we felt when they were on.

Studies done around the chemical oxytocin[7] that's released in the brain and body in men during an orgasm; show that for a woman that exact same chemical oxytocin can be released in her brain and body through deep, meaningful, fun, emotional conversation. Guys, foreplay happens for your bride when you look into her eyes and value what she's saying.

By and large, a lot of men who complain about dead beds because they're not getting enough sex from their wives, only view her as selfish or naïve for not meeting his needs. But answering the following questions may reveal a clue to the sex deprivation he is experiencing in his marriage: Do you value your wife's opinion? Do her thoughts matter to you? Are her feelings so important that when she's upset the game stops, the television goes off, the laptop is shut down and the cellphone is placed on silent until she's been heard, understood, and in a good place? Or when she's upset, do you choose to go into your man cave and avoid her and pleasure yourself and continue to build walls of isolation?

Here's a good place to throw in another Side Chickology lesson because dead bed marriages are fertile environments for the birthing of infidelity. Often the frustrated husband has met or found some other woman, who he's convinced is everything his wife is not, and this Side Chick is willing to give him whatever he wants.

I've got a description for that kind of relationship – Make-Believe. It's all a farce. You know why? Because if that other woman was as good to her husband as she is to you, she would have a better marriage or she'd be married. If you were as good to your wife as you are to her, your wife would be happy and she'd be open to you head to toe! Instead of continuing that fantasy world relationship, work diligently and effectively on your real-world relationship. The reality is, if you have the time and energy to invest in an affair, you have the time and energy to invest in your marriage.

I'd be remiss if I didn't close this section by acknowledging the fact that there are many women who are experiencing a dead bed because the husband is the one that doesn't want to have sex. I say to you that you have to get into counseling to find out what the root is that's causing the fruit of his disinterest or disengagement.

There are a number of other things that can contribute to a dead bed, and I'd like to group the next three contributors as 4. *Triple A – Abuse, Adultery, and Abandonment.* Sometimes marriages are distanced and even devastated by abuse, adultery, or abandonment. Although I don't think any of these things should ever be tolerated, especially abuse because of how dangerous it could ultimately be, there are marriages that have survived each of these things at some level.

Abuse can be emotional, physical, verbal, sexual, and even the abuse of children. Whenever any kind of abuse exists in a family or marriage, distance is a natural result because we seek protection and safety through space.

Abandonment and neglect are different forms of abuse. When someone that you were depending on and expecting to keep their promise and commitment to you, leaves you emotionally or literally that obviously creates distance in the relationship.

Although abandonment and abuse are very painful and challenging matters, the purpose of this book is to address the issue of infidelity, so I'd like to spend a little more time addressing that here.

Now ironically there are times when a marriage experiences infidelity even while there's plenty of sex *in* the marriage. This is not a diagnosis as I'm not qualified to give one, but that could mean that the person is a sex addict and no amount of sex will ever satisfy him/her. When that's the case, there's always a deeper meaning behind the person's sexual addiction, because sex is one way that people medicate deep emotional pain and emptiness. Keep in mind, that even when a marriage is experiencing regular sex, that doesn't mean that the marriage is experiencing a regular amount of connection and intimacy. What that marriage may have is a sexual agreement that creates and honors appointments to perform sexual duties, but the connection on an emotional level is gone.

RECOVERING FROM THE ABYSS OF AN AFFAIR

Debby Wade, a sex & marriage therapist based in Grapevine, Texas[8], once shared with me that the data shows that between 75 to 80% of marriages that experience infidelity, survive. Now I'm not encouraging anyone to test that statistic by crossing the line, but I do want to give hope to people who automatically assume that their marriage is over because of it.

When something as devastating as infidelity rears its ugly head in a marriage, we need a plan to recover from it. Here's help that I think is priceless. John Gottman says the following steps are critical for recovering from marital infidelity[9]:

1. ATONE – There must be an acknowledgment and full responsibility taken on the part of the unfaithful spouse for their behavior. This acknowledgment is critical to the rebuilding of trust, as is a complete severance of all ties to the person involved in the extra-marital relationship. Whatever it takes. No turning back. Accountability is also critical here because oftentimes people who have become deeply entangled in an affair, can't untangle themselves without external support and boundaries.

2. ATTUNE – A fresh and new commitment to the prioritization of the marriage is important at this point. Learning how to work through conflict in healthy ways is also vital here. This is where a re-connection on an emotional level takes place. Be patient, however, this takes significant time, but don't lose heart. Your marriage's direction toward healing is more important than the pace in which it seems to be happening.

3. ATTACH – The process of attuning must eventually lead to the bedroom. There must be sexual intimacy that is mutually pleasurable for the relationship to continue to rebuild. In every marriage, regular sex protects and connects. A lot of the healing has to happen where the illness was discovered. Again, it doesn't start in the bed, but atonement and attunement lead to this level of attachment. (*However, for medical safety purposes, a time of celibacy in the marriage is usually necessary while medical testing is done to rule out sexually transmitted diseases. Also a time of celibacy is often necessary for emotional healing as well.)

So now that we've looked at a number of reasons why people fall out of love, let's look at the things we need to do to fall in love *again*.

Make appreciation and praise a regular part of your relationship. Every marriage can benefit greatly from having intentional times when you express what you love, like, and appreciate about each other. This can be done both spontaneously and systemically. It's been said that it takes at least 10 positive words to over-ride the damage of 1 negative word. If that statistic is true, imagine the emotional deficit with which we live in our relationships simply because we don't celebrate, praise, and appreciate each other.

The absence of gratitude creates an environment of frustration, disappointment, and pain in our marriages. Period. Not being grateful makes happiness and contentment impossible.

<u>Practicing the Principle of Honor.</u> Honoring and protecting our marriages is something that has to be done both privately and publicly. In other words, we can't just say and do the right things when we're with our spouse, we must honor and protect our spouses when we're not with them.

Our conversations should always communicate to people a love and respect and commitment to our spouse, even in their absence.

Bring up your wife and bring up your husband in conversations with people you meet and people you work with. Bring them up. No one that you interact with on a regular basis should be surprised that you're married and they shouldn't have to look at your ring finger to determine it.

I believe that not ever mentioning your husband or wife in conversations is a form of unfaithfulness, because even if people know that you're married, they may assume that your perpetual silence regarding your spouse is an indication of ingratitude or dissatisfaction in your marriage.

Conversely, when you bring up your husband and your wife and you speak of him or her often and in a good light, it communicates marital solidarity to those around you. Frankly, that solidarity needs to be communicated even during times when it doesn't really exist. That's not lying, that's just wisdom. It's protection from the heightened possibility of inappropriate conversations with someone else. That is called verbal infidelity, and it can be fostered when we never have anything positive to say about our spouse.

Verbal fidelity is honoring and speaking well of our spouses in their presence and in their absence, focusing on their strong suits and their highest attributes. It is highlighting those things about them that are good and honorable, and giving thanks for it to them, to God, and to others.

Make dating each other a weekly event. My friend and author, Johnny Parker[10] often says, "Any couple that's not regularly courting each other are headed to court." Dating brings fun back into the relationship like nothing else. Go out together. See Chapter 11 under "Play Together" for more on dating in marriage.

Ask revelatory questions that will help you to love effectively. Find out what they really love and what makes them feel loved the most. Don't assume you know your mate so well that you don't need to periodically check in to see if you know exactly what makes them really feel loved. But it's important that you only ask this question if you intend to use it to help you love your spouse and not harm them by using it against them.

 Pray for and with each other. Intercede for and with each other. This produces spiritual intimacy. Besides, we need God and we can't make it without Him.

Share your feelings with each other. Emotionally safe relationships have safety in sharing feelings without attacking or judging each other.

Respond positively to promptings to move closer to each other. Every now and then you'll get a "prompting" to just go and hug your spouse, or to pray together, or to call him or her to tell them that you love them, or to express some sort of appreciation, or text them a love note. Act on those promptings. Overcome the feelings of fear and worrying about rejection, and just do the right thing when you're prompted. When you're the recipient of those unexpected moments of love, always try to receive them positively, unless there's been an injury in the relationship that hasn't been acknowledged or addressed. In that case, use the moment to try to heal the wound.

Always own your stuff. If you mess up, fess up. Period. Stop trying to justify wrongdoing without apologizing for the pain it caused even if it was unintentional. Own your stuff.

Fight Fair. Deal with the issue before you and resist the urge to bring ammunition based on old stuff. The tools of a fair fight are given in Chapter 12 of this book. Please review the LUVAFA tool and the SBI tool. On the other hand, the enemies of a fair fight that will do deep damage are shaming, screaming, and swearing.

SHAMING: When you say hurtful, shameful things about your spouse, oftentimes that are unnecessary and aren't even related to the situation. For example, the two of you are talking about a disagreement over something regarding one of the children, and you say in anger, "What do you know about parenting, you can't even keep a job for more than 6 months!" Those stabs go deep and they have to be eliminated.

SCREAMING: Once you start raising your voice in an argument with your spouse it is time to pause and take a break, go to your neutral corners, and resume the discussion when you're both in a better place emotionally. Go for a prayer walk. Go get some Starbucks. Go listen to some good music. Go watch some good preaching and teaching. Read something helpful on marriage or conflict. Relax and pray.

My friend, whenever you yell at or scream at your spouse the volume of your words sends a chill through your entire house. Even the children are frightened by it.

SWEARING: You should never curse at your spouse or call them profane names. Words are powerful. We have to understand that we have the power of life and death in our mouths, and stewarding that power in an argument is terribly important. To curse at your spouse is the ultimate disrespect and disregard. It's verbal abuse. If you're mad enough to yell and cuss, it's time to end the conversation. (This is very important. If your spouse tries to walk away because they're getting so upset that they're liable to say something harmful, don't follow them around and incite them. Give them time and trust that they'll return when things cool off.)

Get Counseling. Just about every time I tell couples that they need to get counseling, they almost always say, "Been there, done that Rev." The reason why the counseling recommendation is often blown off, is because couples think they can go to a 45-60 minute counseling session once a week, and do next to nothing the rest of the week to improve their marriage. So, after they do that 5 or 6 times they stop going. That's unreasonable. Marriage takes work and intentionality, and it especially takes a great deal of time, work, and healing when there's been infidelity.

People often give Vicki and I praise for our marriage, especially when they see our date posts on social media. I'm telling you there is no façade about it. We are really connected and in love with one another, but we have had to work on our marriage, and in our marriage and on ourselves for *years* to get to this point. And we're still working on it.

CONCLUSION

With the support of my wife, the prayers of many, and the aid of God Almighty, I have poured my heart, mind, and soul into this work and I pray that this tool becomes a treasure for countless people.

To every person holding this book who's been living in a deeply wounded and lonely marriage, your story is not over yet. I pray that you will devote yourself to giving your marriage story the ending you know is best for everyone connected to you. Trust me, it's worth fighting for.

Blessings,

Keith A. Battle

ENDNOTES

Introduction
[1] http://www.statisticbrain.com/infidelity-statistics/
This link may require a paid subscription to the site to access it.)

[2]The State of Affairs: Rethinking Infidelity by Esther Perel, pg. 18.
Harper Collins Publishers Copyright 2017.

Chapter 1
[1] https://www.verywell.com/understanding-attention-deficit-
disorders-216
2405?utm_term=attention+deficit+disorders&utm_content=p1-
main-1-
title&utm_medium=sem&utm_source=google_s&utm_
campaign=adid-
81e50260-5f24-4e04-8c88-a0905881b182-0-ab_gsb_ocode-
12487&ad=
semD&an=google_s&am=broad&q=attention+deficit+disorders&o
=12487&qsrc=999&l=sem&askid=81e50260-5f24-4e04-8c88-a090
5881b182-0-ab_gsb

[2] The Holy Bible, New Living Translation. Tyndale House
Publishers, Inc. Carol Stream, Illinois copyright 2009.

[3]Arista Records, by Raydio featuring Ray Parker, Jr. Released April
11, 1981.

Chapter 2

[1] Six Levels of Communication Video by Gary Smalley - https://www.youtube.com/watch?v=2-flox2qQrY

[2] http://johnnyparker.com

[3] https://www.today.com/health/ivillage-2013-married-sex-survey-results-
1D80245229

[4] https://www.huffingtonpost.com/entry/sex-problems-that-could-tank-a-
marriage_us_58dadd02e4b054637062ff98

[5] https://www.webroot.com/us/en/home/resources/tips/digital-family-life/
internet-pornography-by-the-numbers

[6] Ecclesiastes 1:8. The NKJV Study Bible. Copyright 2007 by Thomas Nelson, Inc.

Chapter 3

[1] Proverbs 18:22. The Holy Bible, New International Version pg. 635. Copy
right 2005 by Zondervan.

[2] Genesis 2:21-25. New King James Study Bible pg. 8. Copyright 2007 by
Thomas Nelson, Inc.

[3] https://en.wikipedia.org/wiki/Richard_A._Cohen

[4] Galatians 6:7. Holy Bible, New Living Translation. Copyright 2007 by
Tyndale House Foundation.

Chapter 4

[1] https://www.verywell.com/what-is-cognitive-dissonance-2795012

[2] Genesis 16:2. The Holy Bible, New International Version. Copyright 1984
by International Bible Society.

[3]Genesis 16:4. Ibid.

Chapter 5
[1]2 Samuel 11:3. The Holy Bible, New Living Translation. Copyright 2009 Tyndale House Publishers.

[2] http://www.metrolyrics.com/tryin-to-love-two-lyrics-william-bell. html

Chapter 6
[1]https://www.biblestudytools.com/nlt/proverbs/ passage/?q=proverbs+5:3-14

[2]The State of Affairs: Rethinking Infidelity by Esther Perel, pgs. 55-57, Harper Collins Publishers. Copyright 2017.

[3]Focus on the Family – "Infidelity: The Road to Recovery, Where to Start." Bible Application Study.

Chapter 7
[1]Focus on the Family – "Infidelity: The Road to Recovery, Where to Start." Bible Application Study.

[2] https://www.ncbi.nlm.nih.gov/pmc/articles/PMC4240051/

[3] https://www.biblegateway.com/ passage/?search=Malachi+2%3A11-16& version=NLT

[4]https://www.biblegateway.com/ passage/?search=Proverbs+6%3A27-35& version=NLT

5 https://www.verywellfamily.com/psychological-effects-of-divorce-on-kids-4140170

Chapter 8
[1]https://www.biblegateway.com/passage/?search=Galatians+6%3A7& version=GNT

Chapter 9

[1]https://www.biblegateway.com/
passage/?search=Genesis+2%
3A21-25&version=NLT

[2] https://www.goodreads.com/quotes/249554-the-woman-was-
made-of-
a-rib-out-of-the

[3] https://www.youtube.com/watch?v=PucO0w-HU70

[4]https://www.biblegateway.com/passage/?search=1+Corinthians+
11%3A3&version=NLT

Chapter 10

[1]https://www.biblegateway.com/passage/?search=Psalm+40%3A1-3&
version=NKJV

[2]https://www.biblegateway.com/passage/?search=Romans+5%3A8&
version=NLT

[3]https://genius.com/Luther-vandross-any-love-lyrics

Chapter 11

[1]Leading With A Limp by Dr. Dan B. Allender. WaterBrook Press
pg. 14. Copyright 2006

[2]Worthy Of Her Trust: What You Need to Do to Rebuild Sexual
Integrity and Win Her Back by Stephen Arterburn and Jason
B. Martinkus. Kindle Edition location 238, Waterbrook Press,
Copyright 2014.

Chapter 13

[1]https://www.biblegateway.com/
passage/?search=Proverbs+5%3A15-20&
version=NLT

[2]https://www.biblegateway.com/
passage/?search=1+Corinthians+7%3A1-5
&version=NLT

[3]https://www.biblegateway.com/

passage/?search=Song+of+Solomon+1%3A2
&version=NIV

[4]https://www.biblegateway.com/
passage/?search=Song+of+Solomon+1%3A3
&version=NLT

[5]https://www.biblegateway.com/
passage/?search=Song+of+Solomon+1%3A12
&version=NLT

[6]https://www.biblegateway.com/
passage/?search=Song+of+Solmon+2%3A2-4+
&version=NLT

[7]https://www.biblegateway.com/
passage/?search=Song+of+Solmon+2%3A6
&version=NLT

[8]https://www.biblegateway.com/
passage/?search=Song+of+Solomon+2%
3A13&version=NLT

[9]https://www.biblegateway.com/
passage/?search=Song+of+Solmon+2%3A16
-17&version=NLT

[10]https://www.biblegateway.com/
passage/?search=Song+of+Solmon+4%3A9
&version=NLT

[11]https://www.biblegateway.com/
passage/?search=Song+of+Solmon+4%3A
11-16&version=NLT

[12]https://www.biblegateway.com/
passage/?search=Song+of+Solmon+1%3A
15-16&version=NLT

[13]https://www.biblegateway.com/
passage/?search=Song+of+Solmon+7%3A1&version=NLT

Chapter 14

[1]https://www.meierclinics.com/Levy

[2]https://www.gottman.com/blog/husband-can-influential-accept-influence/

[3]https://www.gottman.com/blog/emotionally-intelligent-husbands-key-
lasting-marriage/

[4]https://www.businessinsider.com/the-secret-to-a-happy-marriage-may-be-
an-emotionally-intelligent-husband-2016-10

[5]https://www.businessinsider.com/the-secret-to-a-happy-marriage-may-be-
an-emotionally-intelligent-husband-2016-10

[6]https://www.evanmarckatz.com/blog/understanding-men/a-good-man-is-
hard-to-find-only-35-of-men-are-emotionally-intelligent/

[7]https://verilymag.com/2016/05/oxytocin-sex-differences-women-hormones-
bonding-sex-trust

[8]https://www.linkedin.com/in/debby-wade-77971b37

[9]https://www.gottman.com/blog/learning-to-love-again-after-an-affair/

[10]https://johnnyparker.com/about/

ABOUT THE AUTHOR

Keith Battle and his wife Vicki have been married for 30 years. They have 3 adult children and one grandchild. Keith counsels married couples and consults with business and church leaders. He's the Senior Pastor of Zion Church. He serves as the Chaplain of the Washington Wizards, and on the weekends, he can be heard on his Weekly Wisdom Radio Broadcast in the DMV area, and world-wide via Zion Church's Live Stream. You can also hear him weekly on The Keith Battle Podcast.